BUDGET MARKETING

How to Start & Market an Online Business with Little or Zero Marketing Budget

I0471447

by GabrielaTaylor

ISBN - 978-1490960338

Get FREE Content Marketing Plan Template
downloadable from my website:
www.gabrielataylor.com

Legal Notice

The publisher and author have strived to be as accurate and complete as possible in the creation of this book. The contents within are accurate and up to date at the time of writing however the publisher accepts that due to the rapidly changing nature of the Internet some information may not be fully up to date at the time of reading.

Whilst all attempts have been made to verify information provided in this publication, the Publisher assumes no responsibility for errors, omissions, or contrary interpretation of the subject matter herein. Any perceived slights of specific people or organizations are unintentional. This book makes no guarantees of success or implied promises. The strategies detailed in these pages will work, but are dependent on the work ethic and diligence of the reader.

All Rights Reserved

Dedicace

This book is dedicated to all the bloggers, tweeters, and pinners who make the Internet what it is today. Through your input you open up the web as an amazing resource for all, bring value to others and contribute to a better Internet.

TABLE OF CONTENTS

ABOUT THE AUTHOR

Gabriela Taylor (www.gabriela-aylor.com) is an internationally educated Global Online Marketing Strategist and Consultant who's worked with some of the world's biggest brands in Telecommunications, Retail, Lifestyle and Advertising.

A recognized expert and specialist in Social Networking, Mobile Marketing and Search Engine Optimization, she is fluent in 7 languages, has lived and worked in many countries throughout the world and has experience of implementing successful web-presence strategies for both startup and large established organizations. She is fully certified in Google AdWords and Analytics and furthermore is an experienced coach and business mentor.

She is the founder of Global & Digital (www.globalndigital.com), a publishing company specializing in assisted self-publishing, marketing and mentoring for independent authors. Global & Digital specialise in helping published or first-time unpublished authors take their work to market in digital, print and audio formats. Gabriela is also actively involved in other businesses offering Online and Offline Marketing services, Cross-Cultural business

consultancy and has published several industry related
books:

- *Pinterest Marketing: The Ultimate Guide*
- *Socialize To Monetize: How to Run Effective Social Media Campaigns Across the Top 25 Social Networking Sites*
- *Building and Marketing Your Business with Google*
- *Zero Budget Marketing: How to Start & Market an Online Business with Little or Zero Marketing Budget*
- *Advertising in a Digital Age: Best Practices for AdWords and Social Media Advertising*
- *Globalize to Monetize: Taking Your Online Business to New Markets*
- *Plan, Create, Optimize, Distribute: Your Strategic Roadmap to Content Marketing Success*
- *Targeting Your Market: Marketing Across Generations, Cultures & Gender*
- *Mobilize to Monetize: The Fast Track to Effective Mobile Marketing*
- *Tumblr for Business: The Ultimate Guide*

Connect with the Author:

Website – www.gabrielataylor.com

Twitter – www.twitter.com/globalndigital

Pinterest – www.pinterest.com/taylorgabriela

Linkedin – www.linkedin.com/in/gabrielataylor

Facebook – www.facebook.com/globalndigital

INTRODUCTION

While traditional marketing and advertising strategies are still relevant, the Internet has made it much easier to build and market your business at much lower costs. More businesses are creating an online presence due to the revolutionary Power of the Internet to connect them with their customers. With the Internet, you can now lower your cost of operations, easily find new customers and improve your business bottom line. There are more than 2 billion Internet users across the globe, who serve as a great pool of potential customers.

Obviously, **your business cannot cater to all the Internet users, but you will be exposed to more customers than if you didn't have an online presence.** There are low barriers to entry in building an online business. This makes it easy for even the smallest business to set up successfully and to manage a profitable business. Admittedly, the initial setting up might require some investment on your part, but this is much lower than setting up a brick-and-mortar store. Some of the basic costs that you will incur include development of a website, search engine optimization, and perhaps online advertising. As you settle in your business, you will learn how to manage these aspects of running an online business, thereby saving a significant amount of money.

Finding the right customers and connecting with them to establish a long-term relationship is important to every business. However, this can be costly and can negatively affect a business' bottom line. Yet the Internet is a social community, in which you can easily find where your customers are, connect with them and convert them into buying clients. Businesses with an online presence are leveraging the power of social media networks such as Facebook, Twitter, LinkedIn, Google+, YouTube and Pinterest to engage with their customers. Using these effective platforms costs nothing, yet the returns can be significant for both big and small businesses. **You will be surprised by just how many people are willing to do business with you when they can find you online**.

Marketing and advertising take up a large chunk of a business' budget. However the Internet has made it so easy to market your brand and product offering at a much lower cost and even for free. Most of the marketing channels are free to use or will not cost you much compared to offline advertising, online advertising does not require heavy investment. The ads are targeted and are more likely to have a greater ROI (return on investment). Today, it is possible to boost your marketing campaign by developing and giving out incentives that do not cost you anything, but help you to reach out to your target audience. Internet technology has made it possible to reach out to a larger audience by allowing you to create webinars and videoconferences at almost no cost at all. In this way, you can market your products and at the same time connect with your audiences regardless of their location.

The Internet literally offers thousands of free solutions that will support your marketing and advertising campaign. Some, naturally, are better than others and some may appear to be free at first but have hidden costs attributed to them if you want to use them for effective commercial purposes. There are however many fantastic free tools out there that I have tried and tested and it is definitely possible to build and market your business for ZERO COST using these tools. Why pay for online tools when there are fantastic free ones available that will massively benefit your business and that cost you absolutely nothing? This book will take you through some of the best tools available, will provide you with the top tips you need to succeed and will also give you a host of useful links to online resources.

Chapter 1
10 REASONS WHY YOUR LOCAL BUSINESS NEEDS AN ONLINE PRESENCE

More and more businesses are establishing an online presence. This is because customers are increasingly going online to access the goods and services they need. Also online business-to-business transactions have become a common trend. Going online brings your business to more people that you would expect a brick-and-mortar store to. When you strategically launch your online business, you will not only gain greater visibility but also improve your return on investment. Here are 10 reasons why your local business should establish an online presence:

1. Customer Accessibility

Consider this: a survey conducted by WebVisible & Nielsen showed that **3 out of 4 people use the major search engines to find local businesses**. This means that if someone is looking for a local restaurant, a shoe repair shop, a specialty bookshop or any local service, 75% of the time they will use a search engine such as Google to find this business. As such if you are not online, it means that up to 75 percent of your potential customers are not finding you.

However, what if they could find you and see the range of products and services you are offering? This can go a long way in boosting your customer base and your business profits too.

Unlike the brick-and-mortar shops that have to close at some point in the day, the Internet opens 24/7. By having an online presence, your business will go on regardless of the time of day. Customers will still be able to look around your online shop and your product offering and make purchases. This essentially maximizes the business hours so that you are operating a 24-hour business without the need to be physically present. By being open for longer you will be surprised at just how much you will be able to improve on the sales numbers and overall business revenues.

2. Wider Audience

Over 2 billion people have access to the Internet today. This global audience presents a lucrative opportunity as prospective customers. If you have the capacity or the long-term plans, you can sell your goods and services to people in other countries. Instead of setting up a brick-and-mortar shop in every country or geographical location that you want to reach, you simply need to set up a virtual shop that anyone can access.

Gaining an online presence for your local business is made easier by free online tools and mobile & web applications that your customers can use to find out what you are offering. Because people are looking online first before they can make purchasing decisions, it means that those local businesses that have an online presence are attracting more customer inquiries. Any business knows that inquiries, even though they do not lead to an immediate sale, are not necessarily a bad thing. It is through answers to inquiries that you are able to pitch to your local customers. But without an online presence you just might not have as many prospects to pitch to as you would like.

3. Customer Reviews

Both online and offline businesses rely on 'word of mouth' as one of the most significant channels of their marketing. But as an offline business, 'word of mouth' reviews by customers can only reach so many people, usually a customer's close friends and family. Yet an online presence allows customers to post reviews about your business and thousands of potential customers will access the reviews and your product offering. Of course, reviews can make or break your business; you need to offer the best services and customer support for your business to receive great reviews. Having an online presence offers your customers a viable platform to undertake 'word of mouth' marketing on your behalf. Many studies have shown that potential clients often look through reviews before they can purchase a product or service offering from you.

4. Brand Building and Visibility

Brand visibility means making your brand known to potential customers. As a brick-and-mortar business, you might be surprised to find out that just a few people know about your business brand. But by bringing your business online you become more visible to the people that matter the most: potential customers and the media. The media, whether social or mainstream can play an important role in promoting and marketing your business, but you have to let them know that your business exists in the first place.

Brand building means building trust between your business and these potential customers. Bringing your business online serves as an effective way for prospects to see what you have to offer and what your business is all about. Remember that for almost all customers, "seeing is believing". An online presence allows your prospects to see whether you are the right business to purchase a product or service from. It enable potential clients to compare your offering with that of the competition and it also offers you ample opportunities to tell the client why you are better than the competition.

5. Marketing and Selling Made Easy

It is a known fact that people do not like to be sold to and businesses do not usually like to come off as being too pushy. However, the Internet provides an ideal platform for businesses to effectively market and sell their products without having to apply too much pressure on the customers. By creating great informational and marketing copy for your product offering, you allow the customer to make an informed and relaxed decision. When done strategically, online marketing can be effective in building rapport between you and your customers and establishing long-term partnerships.

Online marketing also allows you to present your offer in a way that is appealing to your target audience. You not only sell them your product offering but you can easily give your audience incentives that they can access easily. For example as part of your marketing campaign, you can give out free digital products such as ebooks and white papers at almost no cost at all. Compare this to offline marketing where you would have to print out these incentives or give incentives that cost you so much.

6. Reduced Cost of Operation

Having your business online will greatly reduce your cost of doing business. Admittedly, the initial cost of setting up will cost you a significant amount, but the long-term benefits far outweigh these initial costs. The best thing about setting up online is that once you set up, the costs begin to reduce as you enjoy an improved business bottom line. With an online presence, you may eliminate costs such as customer support, office space, marketing research and advertisement as various online tools can help you automate most of these.

7. Affordable Infrastructure

One of the apprehensions that businesses have when going online is related to payment and delivery, however there are plenty platforms and solutions available to you to make business transactions much easier. First, your website will be protected by Secure Socket Layer encoding that secures the transactions between you and your customers and will warn you in the event of any security threats to your site. Additionally, you will have access to a large number of online merchant payment options such as PayPal and others through which customers can make easy payments just from your own website.

8. Connecting with Customers

More and more businesses are looking for innovative ways of connecting with their customers, without breaking the bank. The Internet offers the perfect opportunity for businesses to find where their target audience is and to engage them.

Once you bring your business online, you can connect with your target audience in many ways. You can send them personalized emails about product offerings, offer them informative articles on your site, or create entertaining and educational videos. Additionally, you can develop interactive applications to engage your customers with your business or provide value on forums and social networking platforms.

9. Effective Tracking of Progress

Sometimes offline businesses do not have a cost effective and reliable method of tracking progress. Yet with an online business, you can track, monitor and measure just about any metric that is important to your business. There are both free tools such as Google Analytics and commercial ones that will allow you to measure your online business progress at any time and receive instant results.

10. No Inventory Required

There are companies that do drop-shipping for you so that you, unlike an offline business, do not have to keep any inventory. Drop-shipping companies are suppliers of the products that customers buy from your site. These companies simply ship the product ordered to your customers without you needing to source for the availability of that product and to go through shipping logistics. This can eliminate a significant amount of operational costs that you would have otherwise incurred if you kept inventory.

Chapter 2
GETTING STARTED

As you get started with setting up your online business presence, the most important thing to do is to plan, just as you would do with an offline business. You will quickly realize that the online marketplace is very competitive, that new ideas come and are rapidly replaced by others. For you to stay in business you must develop a deliberate plan that will sustain you in spite of the competition and the constantly changing landscape. Here are some steps to take as you plan to bring your business online.

Research Your Online Competition

Competition analysis and research will help you determine what your business is up against. This type of research will give you in depth insights about the profitability of your niche online and what you can do to stand out from the crowd. However, remember that competitor research is only as effective as how well you use and apply the results. Be sure that you analyze your competitors from your target market's point of view. Important areas to analyze include:

Pay Per Click Analysis

Search engine advertising analysis of your competitors will show you the type of advertisements they are launching, the click through rates and the effectiveness of their ads. First, you need to identify who your competiton is. You may think that it is just one company when there are ten more that have a similar service or product offering as you. You will also want to analyze how savvy the competition is in terms of their website, the content they offer there, as well as their social media pages. How are they using retargeted ads and are they leveraging pay per click best practices. Consider using **Google Alerts** and social media platforms to stay abreast with any changes in terms of paid advertising.

Consider the type of messages that they are putting out to their target audience. Are their paid search ads compelling, unique and have the same or different message as your business? In addition, what is their target audience? The answers to these questions will help you determine whether you can improve the message to your target audience and therefore create better ads.

Keyword Analysis

Here are some tips on what to do when looking for your competitors' targeted search terms:

1. Use a keyword analysis tool to find out the words that your competitor is using in their landing and home pages. The words or terms that they use the most are likely to be their targeted search terms.

2. Create a list of these search terms and go back to the list when you start to develop your own site. The idea here is not to copy the exact keywords the competition is using, but to have insights into what is working and what is not.

3. How well are they using their search terms in their various webpages? If they are focusing on more than five keywords on a page, this is likely that they are not properly optimized at the search engines. This is something that you want to avoid.

4. Next, analyze their Meta (meta description, meta keywords, meta author, meta copyright, etc.) and Title tags. How have they written these and how have they placed their keywords. Is their technique effective in making them visible at the search engines? Although meta tags do not have a significant effect on the search engine results, they can still give you an idea as to what the competitor is targeting.

Below I' listed some free tools that you can use to find more about your competitors keywords and their online strategy.

Google Adwords Keyword Planner: can assist you to find key terms and advertisement group ideas that may not occur to you as you design your ad campaign. The platform allows you to enter a word or a group of words and phrases relevant to your business; then the tool will generate related keywords and phrases that you can use for your ads and competitor research.

Freekeywords. wordtracker.com: this platform allows you to track keywords that your competitors may be using in their webpage. You may also use this tool to see the effectiveness of keywords in terms of click through rates, traffic generation and link building.

Keyworddiscovery.com: aggregates search term statistics from all the main search engines. This tool will show you the types of phrases and words that people are using to find services and products as well as the terms that are generating traffic to your competition.

Yahoo Clues: offers you insights into the demographics and attributes of the people using certain search term. The tool also shows you the terms that are related to the terms that people are using. By typing in a key term or phrase, you will see the various trends of that term or phrase. You will also see how popular the keyword is, the searchers' location, income level, gender and age.

Soovle.com: offers you suggestions pertaining to the terms that people use to look for products and services. This tool will help you determine the terms that your competitors' target audience is using to find their ads and sites.

Url.com: allows you to type in URLs of companies and to see their rankings on major site engines including Google, Bing and Yahoo.

Spyfu: enables you to track the phrases that your competition is using; it also shows you the most effective keywords attracting traffic to their site. You may also use this tool to generate your own keywords depending on your budget and business needs.

Quantcast: offers free reports on traffic measurements and audience demographics. This tool is useful if you need comprehensive reports on the traffic trends in your competitors' sites.

Archive.org: this nonprofit, online-based organization hosts Internet sites and serves as a digital library. It offers market researchers like you, resources and a platform to locate online information pertaining to other sites easily.

Alexa: is one of the most utilized tools for all types of web statistics. Using this tool will help you determine indexes such as your competitor rankings in the search engines, the target search terms, the type of traffic the site is attracting locally, nationally and internationally.

Keywordspy.com: allows you to easily determine the competition's pay per click strategy as well as their organic search plan. You can identify the keywords they are using and thus build your own keywords that will make your business more profitable than the competition.

AdWords Analyze Competition Tool: enables you to see how other businesses using the AdWords program are fairing. With this information, you will be in a better position to optimize your ads as you establish your online presence.

Content Analysis

The type of content available on a site demonstrates a business' credibility and competence. In analyzing your competitors' content, you will be able to understand their strengths and weaknesses and to gain an edge. Some questions you may want to ask are whether the competitors' home pages have relevant and important information for their target market. Is this content useful and reliable to interest their target audience? You also want to see if there is any information that they might have left out that is important to potential customers. How strategically have they placed the most important information and how well have they designed their titles, meta descriptions, anchor texts and keywords?

Benefits Analysis

A benefits analysis entails research on the benefits that your competitors offer their target audience. These may be overtly stated or implied; this shows you the competition's competitive advantage or their USP (unique selling points or propositions). You want to see how they are using their sites to promote their products and services and how site users are responding to this. All this information will help you determine your own unique selling points and how you will position these and make them visible to your target audience.

Graphic Design Analysis

As you prepare to design your own website, you want to see what your competition is offering in terms of their web layout. This will give you an insight into the type of audience they may be targeting, and whether they have attractive and uncluttered sites. **Remember that site users consider a website's design to be a mark of credibility or lack of it.** Additionally, take into consideration how effectively their site design helps in promoting and selling their products and services. Lastly, is their site easy to use? Write down the areas of improvement and apply them to your own site.

In addition to the website outlook, it is a good idea to analyze how functional your competitors' site is. Functionality is determined by factors such as the availability of widgets and plug-ins that make it easy for visitors to use the site. You also want to determine whether they offer newsletters, an accessible contacts page, and easy to use shopping carts. Also, is the site optimized to be searchable at the main search engines?

Pricing Analysis

As you plan to bring your business online, it is important to know what others are charging for similar products and services. Although other factors may also determine how you price your offerings, knowing the prevailing prices will give your pricing strategy a bearing. Look out for how your competitors have bundled their offerings to attract customers to spend money on these offerings. Is there anything that you can learn or improve with regard to their pricing strategy? Can you compete based on price and still remain profitable? As you analyze the pricing, you also want to see if there is an opportunity for business-to-business collaboration. This is especially true for small businesses that are coming online into a niche dominated by big businesses. This way you can strategically work with and not against your competitors.

Choose a Business Domain

Now that you plan to establish your online presence, it is important that you choose a name for your website. A domain name is the name that you and your customers will use to refer to your website. Getting a domain name entails choosing a suitable name and registering it with the ICANN organization. You will need a domain name registrar or provider to obtain the name and for them to register this name with the ICANN. Registration for a domain name will typically cost you between $10 and $40. This will allow you to use the domain name for a year after which you must renew it and pay the applicable fee. While some web hosts will register the domain name for you, it is preferable that you use a domain name registrar who will automatically do this for you.

GoDaddy is one of the best domain name providers. It is reliable and has been in the industry long enough to offer economical packages for small and large businesses. It will cost you $1. 99 for non-popular domain names and $9. 99 for popular names with .com or .org extensions. The company offers web-hosting services for about $4. 74 monthly. GoDaddy also provides dedicated and virtual server packages.

While choosing a domain name for your business, here are several factors to take into consideration:

1. Go for the **.com** or **.org** domain name extensions. These are generally considered professional and will exude a level of credibility for your business online. If you are looking to target a specific market based in a specific country, then you may want to use a local top-level domain such as . au for Australia, . de for Germany, . za for South Africa, . co. uk for the UK and so on.

2. Try finding a unique domain name that will identify well with your business. Unique domain names may cost you more but they will go a long way in differentiating you from your competition. Choose a domain name that has a single spelling to ensure that potential customers do not misspell this name.

3. If possible, keep the domain name short; this will add the "stickiness factor" to your domain name so that site visitors always remember this name and easily tell others about it.

4. When deciding between plural or singular domain names, choose the one that is most sensible to your business. Even better, consider buying both the singular and plural names and then redirect one to the other.

5. Purchase or choose domain names that have a keyword related to your business. This ensures that your site URL is appropriately optimized for the search engines. It is a good idea to make use of industry or niche market jargon; this often assures potential visitors that they will find exactly what they are looking for on your site.

6. Choose a domain name that will attract Type-In traffic. Type-In traffic is the traffic generated when site visitors get

directly to your site by typing your URL in their web browser. The best domain names for type-In traffic are those that have an exact match with your business or brand name or a keyword rich. These types of domain names will also give you some competitive advantage at the search engines.

Free vs. Paid Domains

You can choose to have a free or paid domain. For a Free Domain you will not pay anything; you simply choose the domain name from free domain providers and find a web host. The disadvantage of free domains is that they are essentially sub-domains that are part of a larger domain (e.g. yoursite.wordpress.com). If something goes wrong with the main domain, so will your free sub-domain. You risk losing your data.

Paid Domains are arguably a better choice for businesses. Domain names in this category range from as little as $10 annually to thousands of dollars, depending on the value of that domain name. The advantage of paid for domains is that you can have a domain name that reflects your business brand. The name is independent and thus you have more control over your files and contents. Remember to renew your paid for domain each year; if you do not, someone else will buy it.

Choose a Web-Host

Like domain names you may choose to have free or commercial (paid for) web-hosting services. There are numerous web-hosts online offering free hosting services. Equally, you will find web-hosts who charge a fee to host your website. There is no perfect web-host. Just because you pay a lot of money to have your site hosted, does not mean that you are guaranteed to receive better services. This is why it is important to go with web-hosts who are better known, instead of obscure hosts. On the contrary, if you pay little or nothing for your hosting services, you cannot expect superior services and support. Most major domain providers will offer you a web-hosting plan. Essentially, you need to buy a web-hosting plan and then receive a free domain name.

Advantages and Disadvantages of Free Web-Hosting

Free web-hosts provide you with a fixed bandwidth and space to publish your site, usually in exchange for advertisement space. Some free web-hosts include Google and local ISP providers; the greatest advantage with free web-hosting services is that you will not incur any costs and because you are just starting out, you have the space to experiment with your website at no cost. However, with free web-hosting you get very limited space and bandwidth, thus you cannot install too many widgets software. The domain name you receive from a free web-host will most likely not reflect your business and will be too long. You will also be limited in terms of designing the outlook of your website and there is no back up for your data.

Advantages and Disadvantages of Paid Web-Hosting

With commercial web-hosting services, you will need to invest a small amount in exchange for the services. This is not necessarily a disadvantage given that the amount you pay is minimal compared to the benefits that you receive. You will receive enough space and bandwidth; you can choose whether the hosting provider will place ads on your site. Your data is also backed up and secure, you get access to free software including shopping carts, forums, blogs and much more. You may also use your own domain name. Most web-hosting providers will offer you a free domain name when you purchase a web-hosting plan with them. As a business, it is strongly suggested that you invest in a paid web-hosting service.

Some popular domain name providers and web-hosts include:

GoDaddy: offers free domain registration with the purchase of a web-hosting plan. GoDaddy also offers a free website featuring five pages based on their templates. You will get access to blogging widgets, an email account, a photo album tool and 1GB storage.

NameCheap: offers some of the most economical domain name and registration services. They also offer you a free email account, free and personalized domain parking, free domain forwarding and URL transfers. The customer service is also very reliable.

HostGator: like GoDaddy, HostGator offers free domain registration with the purchase of web-hosting services that will cost you $4. 94 monthly. In addition to domain registration, you will receive hosting with unlimited storage and bandwidth. At an extra cost of about $13, you can have access to dedicated servers and unlimited domain names.

BlueHost: offers unlimited web-hosting and free domain. It also provides unlimited email accounts, hosting bandwidth and space, as well as templates and site builders.

1and1: offers both domain registration and hosting services that feature a five-page website. The company also provides a free email account, 2 GB storage, private domain registration for free, as well as free transfer of domains.

Create an Online Business Plan

As you bring your business online, you need a well-written business plan, the same way you would have one for an offline business. An online business plan will guide you in determining your target audience, your competition, your competitive advantage, your market as well as the cost of marketing and promoting your website. Here are some steps to take in creating your online business plan:

Developing Your Unique Selling Points (USP)

To become successful in the highly saturated and competitive online business world, you need to identify your USP (unique selling points) or your competitive advantage. It is important that you determine what business you are in and the attributes that differentiate you from your online competitors.

To identify your USPs start by assessing the abilities, interests and strengths of your business. If you are an entire company, consider you areas of excellence and competence.

These may include your customer service, your turnaround, or any expertise that your team may possess that sets you apart from the competitors. If you are a single-person online business, take into consideration your professional expertise and experience. These are what you will offer your potential customers.

To identify your own USPs and competencies, you may look to what the competition is offering and their areas of competitive advantage. This will help you craft ways of leveraging your expertise to thrive in a competitive marketplace. Remember that your ideas, products and services can be reproduced easily. Find ways to always stay ahead of your competition.

Setting and Clarifying Goals

Clear goals will give you a direction as to where you want to take your online business. It is very easy to get side tracked when you establish an online presence - there are plenty of opportunities, platforms and solutions that will catch your attention. Nevertheless, let your online business plan reflect your goals so that you will stay on course. Establish financial and non-financial goals that take into consideration your marketing plan. An example of **a non-financial goal** can be to reach to a certain population (say the Chinese market) in the next 5 years. **A financial goal** would be something like to increase your business sales revenues from $2 million to $5 million annually. **Remember that as your business progresses, the goals set will continue to change as well.** This means that your business plan will require revisions as you go along.

Customer Analysis

Your business plan needs to show the type of customers you are targeting. **Do not fall into trap of wanting to sell to everybody!** Instead, identify a niche market that will be willing to spend money on the products and service that you offer. Your niche market can be large or small, and this depends on what you are offering. Customers can be individuals, groups or businesses.

Take note that business-to-business customers and transactions are different from business to customer transactions. Thus, you need to be clear whether you will be dealing with business customers, individual customers or both.

As you move online, the attributes of your usual customers will change because people from all over the world will now find your business. Some things to consider when defining your customers include their geographical location, cultural and ethnic dispensation, age, gender, economic conditions and lifestyles. If you are doing business-to-business transactions, consider the size of the companies that you are targeting, the decision-making level of the customers and their buying capacity.

Customer Value

Customer value can be defined as how much a customer is to your business in relation to profits, sales and buying capacity. According to the well-known business guru Jay Abrahams, you can only know how much time and resources to spend on a customer, when you know the combined profits that they will bring to your business. If you are a start-up, determining customer value will largely be experimental or work on approximation to determine the type of customer that you are looking for. However as you get to attract more clients you should begin to identify the most valuable. To calculate customer value:

1. Calculate the average profit for each sale i. e. the total revenues minus marketing, advertising and expenses from fulfilling a service or delivering a product, and then divide the results with the quantity of sales.

2. Next, establish the number of times a customer will buy your offerings over a period of two years or a year.compute the profits that you are likely to make over the course of that one-year or two.

This should give a rough estimation of what the most profitable customer will look to you.

The Marketing Budget

It is one thing to have a fancy website, but another to actually market and promote your website to attract traffic to it. In your business plan, you need to note down the various ways of marketing your website and how much these will cost you. Some of the marketing costs to consider include:

Website Development and Maintenance

Different websites will incur different development and maintenance costs. Some factors that will influence the cost of your site include the availability of widgets, the design, whether it is a dynamic or a static site. In general website development and maintenance expenses can cost you as low as $1,000 or as high as $10,000.

Search Engine Optimization

Directories and search engines will play a significant role as you market your site. Thus, most of your marketing budget will be focused on SEO costs. Search engine traffic is free to generate, but the services of a professional SEO company will be invaluable in actually helping you generate this traffic. Hiring a professional SEO company might cost you as much as $50 to $100 hourly.

Search Advertising/Pay Per Click Advertising

The cost of pay per click advertising campaigns will vary depending on the industry you are in and the amount of traffic you are looking to generate. This may cost you as much as $200 or an upward of $5,000 for the most professional search engine advertising services.

Affiliate Marketing

If you have plans for expansion, then you might want to look into affiliate marketing. Although this is a great way to attract traffic to your site and earn extra income, it will cost you too. The decent affiliate networks will charge you between $50 and $10,000 to get you started. The network will also take about 20-30% commission in the sales revenues you generate from your site selling their products.

Designing the Sales Funnel

A sales funnel is simply a map that shows you the conversion process and buying behavior that your site visitors exhibit as they interact with your site. Designing your sales funnel and incorporating it to your business plan will enable you to develop and optimize your site in a way that makes the conversion and sales process easier for site users and clients.

1. First, establish every step that people take to come through the funnel. Where have these site users come from, what are their attributes (are they high potential customers) and the level that they are on in the purchasing cycle.

2. Determine the types of activities that site visitors are likely to undertake including reading the content, signing up to a news letter, looking at your social media profile, looking at the offers, purchasing, or leave the site.

3. List down the measures to take, to ensure that each of these activities leads to a sale or a subscription.

Chapter 3
DESIGNING YOUR WEBSITE

Designing your website requires that you plan and identify the features you want to appear on your site. It is also important that you establish what you want the website to do for both your long term and short-term business goals. The costs you will incur in designing your site will largely depend on various factors including the method you use to set up, the size of the website, and the features you want to include. Before listing the different ways to build your website, I suggest you have a look at some other things you need to consider when building it.

Designing a Logo

A logo visually and graphically identifies your business or brand. You can easily create your own logo by using platforms such as logomarker.com and cooltext.com, among others. For these platforms, all you need to do is log onto the platform, pick a logo template from the ones available on the platform and then add attributes such as text fonts, colors, spaces and size. Then, go ahead and download your free logo from the platform, allowing it to appear on your website. You can also buy a high-resolution version of the logo to use on business cards and any marketing tools such as banners. However if you can afford to pay for a professional logo, I suggest outsourcing it to someone on fiverr.com where you can pay $5 dollars for a logo or running a logo contest on 99designs.com where it will cost you between $299 and $699 and several designers will submit their logo proposal. As you create your logo, have your target audience in mind; consider their cultural sentiments, their likes, preferences, and the type of brand logo that might appeal to them.

Site Colors

Colors also go a long way in creating the visual appeal and aesthetics that draw site visitors to your site and makes them stay there longer. However, you must be careful how you use colors on your site. Ensure that colors are not too bright or mixed up as this may lower the credibility and professionalism of your business and the site itself. You can use several tools to apply colors on your site. These include ColourLovers, ColourSchemer and Kuler. Kuler is widely used due to the ease in creating and customizing themes. This Adobe color tool is very versatile and once you undertake the quick registration, you can begin to create themes that you can view, retrieve and store in the Mykulerspace personal account. You can create your color themes by choosing colors from the color wheel and then customizing a preferred color from here. You may also import images from Flickr or from your computer and then use the colors on the images to customize a preferred color.

Free Pictures

There are various resources where you can get photos to make your site more visually appealing. These include: **Public Domain Resources** such as Flickr, Google Images, Stockvault and Stock. xchange. These are typically free to use however before using any of their images make sure that the image is labeled as 'free to use or share'. **Right Protected Resources** require you to purchase images to use for specific projects and for certain duration. To use these images you might have to inquire with the original photographer. Due to the limitation in duration and usage, these may not be the best resources to use when looking for images for your site. **Royalty Free Images** are bought, but after you purchased the images you can use them in any way that you wish. However, other people can also buy and use this same image on their websites.

Here is how you can get started building your website:

Use a Template or a Site Builder

Using templates offered by web hosts is one of the easiest ways to build your website. XSitepro is one of the most used site builders due to its ease of use. It is designed primarily for Internet marketers to make the creation of a website easy and to allow Internet marketers to create sites that have the functionality and layout needed to conduct business online. XsitePro allows you to establish AdSense ads within your site, allows for SEO functions, link management, navigation page updating, designing pop ups, establishing redirects and uploading the site.

HostGator also offers a popular site builder that might be more flexible than XsitePro. The site builder is free and here are the steps to use to get you started in creating your website:

Step 1: Select a template for your site from the ones available in the gallery. Choose one that will reflect your business, product offerings and brand.

Step 2: Decide on the types of pages that will feature on your website. HostGator offers a user-friendly interface that allows you to simple choose the page that you want for your site. It also allows you to edit these page layouts to your preference.

Step 3: Format and encode the content that you want featured on your webpages. The process of formatting and encoding is easy. You also have the space to include additional features to your context pages such as RSS feeds, shopping carts and other widgets.

Step 4: Preview your site and then publish it by simply clicking on the publish button. Your website is ready.

Use a Script or CMS

This is the option I use every time I build a new site. The use of customer management systems (CMS) such as WordPress.org, Tumblr or Posterous in creating websites is preferable as you can easily edit and manage the codes on these platforms. Both Tumblr and Posterous for example are very easy platforms to use to create a website. However, WordPress.org is the most commonly used CMS. **The difference between WordPress.org and WordPress.com is that with WordPress.com you can't change the PHP code or upload plugins and your site is hosted for free on their platform. With WordPress.org you need to buy**

your own web-hosting and domain. So I suggest going with WordPress.org and install the WordPress software. And you can configure your WordPress.org content management system to create a website instead of a simple blog. Here are the steps to take in creating a website on WordPress.org:

Step 1: Use an Internet browser to log into the WordPress.org platform. Then, click on the 'New Post' option at the right hand side of the interface. Then, select to create a 'New Page'.

Step 2: Use the WordPress.org editor to create content for the first webpage of your site. You will notice that this editor has similarity to the ordinary word processor with additions such as links, images and rich media.

Step 3: Save the page by clicking the 'Publish' button. Select the 'Settings' options from the left menu and then choose the 'Reading' option from the drop down menu.

Step 4: Select the 'A Static Page' option to choose the name of this first page. Then click on the 'Save Changes' tab to allow the page that you have selected to appear as a static main page that site visitors see when they find your website.

You may continue to create more webpages by clicking on the 'New Page' button at the top of the interface.

Step 5: You may add widgets by going to the 'Appearance' tab on the menu on the left. Then, click on the 'Widgets' option from the drop down menu.

Step 6: Choose the area that you would like the widget to appear. Select the name of the widget and then drag it to the chosen area allowing it to be added to your website.

Step 7: Edit the widget settings by clicking on the widget name. Then, select 'Save' to save these settings.

Step 8: Select the name of your website on the top left side of the interface to preview the changes that you have made on your site. You may go back to the dashboard to add more webpages or to edit the existing ones.

WORDPRESS PLUGINS TO CONSIDER

1. Theme Customization: WordPress.org (free) or StudioPress (paid)

2. SEO Optimization: All In One SEO

The WordPress SEO plug-in allows you to automatically optimize your website for the major search engines. This free tool includes:

a. Support for customized posts

b. Google Analytics integration into your website

c. The use of canonical URLs

d. Automatic customization of titles allowing your target audience to easily find your site

e. Automatic generation of meta tags

3. Shopping Cart: WP e-Commerce or ShopperPress

WP e-Commerce: this is a free and versatile WordPress plug-in that allows you to set up an e-store where you can sell products and services. The plug-in is compatible with any WordPress.org theme and can function properly with other WordPress plug-ins. Additionally it generates meta descriptions as well as RSS feeds for product offerings. Premium upgrades for extra features are available.

ShopperPress: this paid plug-in enables you to create customized product attributes including sizes and colors. The tool is optimized to allow your ecommerce site or website store to have higher rankings at the major search engines. Once you install the ShopperPress shopping cart widget you can easily manage it from the admin section without the need for programming knowledge.

4. Membership Softwares: WishListMember or MemberWing

WishListMember: this tool enables you to customize your WordPress website into a complete membership site. All you need is to upload the widget and your website will have the functions of a membership-based site that features password protected areas and content that is only viewable by members. Other features include easy management of members, integrated system for payment, a shopping cart widget and integration into WordPress. It only costs $97 for one domain or $297 for unlimited domains.

MemberWing: this is a tool that that allows you to create dynamic and search engine optimized membership sites and to add an online storefront from where you can sell information products. You may also integrate your website with other tools such as Aweber that enable you to build an email list or you may also create opt-in lists and offer trial access to premium products for those who do not want to immediately subscribe as members.

5. Mobile Friendly Plugin: WP Mobile Detector

WP Mobile Detector: is a plug-in that notices when a visitor is accessing your site from a mobile phone. This plug-in automatically configures your website so that it is easily accessible from a mobile phone. The plug-in also allows images to be resized within the mobile platform, and content formatting to allow site visitors to have a pleasant experience when using a mobile to navigate your site.

Use a Web-Authoring Program

You can use numerous html wysiwyg (what you see is what you get) editors to create your website; some are free while others are commercial. Each of the web-authoring programs has its own technical requirements for you to create a website.

Dreamweaver: is the most popular web-authoring program for building websites. Here are the basic steps for setting up a website using this application:

Step 1: Install and start your Dreamweaver. Then, define the site by selecting 'Site' and then clicking on the 'New Site' tab. This will enable the Site Definition window to appear; click on 'Advanced' and then 'Local Info' category.

Step 2: Type in your name in the site name field. Identify the root folder path that is stored in your computer. Select the 'Refresh' option to see a list of the local files. Activate the cache option.

Step 3: Enter the URL that you have chosen for your website in the Address field. This will allow Dreamweaver to confirm the links in the website.

Step 4: Select the 'Remote Information' tab and then click on the 'Access' drop down menu to select FTP. In the FT field, enter the name of the remote server that will be hosting your website. You may choose to enter the domain name if it is directed toward the appropriate host.

Step 5: Type in html or a www in the host directory field. This is where your website will be stored. Type in the FTP login information and then examine this connection using the Test button. Ensure that you select the 'Use Passive FTP' tab.

Step 6: Choose the remote server model that you will use from the Testing Server menu. When you set the preferences, select OK to allow for the completion of the set up.

Step 7: To insert attributes such as color, font and font size, go to the work area in Dreamweaver and type in your text. Select the text and then use the 'Properties' tab to choose the various attributes you want to apply on your text.

Step 8: To have images in the site, choose the 'Insert' option and then 'Image. ' Choose any image from your computer files and then insert this into the webpage. You may also use the images 'Properties' tab to apply various attributes to your images including text, names, color and size.

Build It from Scratch

Building your site using HTML allows you greater control in terms of the layout and format of the website. Although the process is manual, it will give you a better understanding of how a website functions. Here are steps to take in creating your website from scratch:

Step 1: Go to 'Start' on your computer and then select' Programs' and then 'Accessories'. Choose the 'Notepad' option or 'Windows'.

Step 2: Type in the html tags for the body and the head sections of the website. Create a title for the first webpage to give site visitors an idea of what the page entails.

Additionally users will see this title when they bookmark your site. Place the title as such <title> and close it by indicating </title>.

Step 3: Create the head section that offers information about the page content that does not show in the webpages. The head tag will influence how the webpage appears.

Step 4: Create the body section, which contains the information that appears on the webpage when users open your website through their web browsers. Pay attention to the webpage body as this is where important textual information, images and videos appear. To do this type in <body> to open the tag and then close the tag by typing in </body>.

Step 5: You can add color and other styles to the page background. Do this by typing <body style="background-color: blue">. It is important that you include quotation marks in the attributes that you are trying to create.

Step 6: Create page links that will link one page on your website to another. As in all other types of tags, link tags have an opening and closing tag. An example of an opening tag would be: <ahref=" http://www. ebusiness.com ">.

Step 7: Save the file in HTML format. Ensure that all tags are closed before saving. You may use any name, but ensure that the name does not have a space in between. It is also advisable that the name ends with . html. This way you will be telling your computer that this is a webpage and that a web browser is required to read it. Avoid using symbols and instead use ordinary numbers and letters.

Step 8: Open the page with your web browser to preview it. To do this, head over to the document's 'File' menu and then choose to 'Open File'. You may continue to tweak the HTML code as you add more features on your website.

Outsource It

Another option is to pay someone to build the website for you. Various web development and design companies will charge you to develop a site for you. You may find these companies online or listed in local directories. You may also use freelance sites such as Elance.com or Odesk.com to find individual web developers and designers from anywhere in the world, who can create a site for you. The advantage of outsourcing your web development needs is that you will save a lot of time than you would were you to create your own website. In addition, unless you are familiar with website creation, expert web developers and designers might be better placed to create a more professional looking website.

Other Important Features of Your Website to Consider

Payment

PayPal: is the most preferred system payment system for Internet marketers and online businesses. It is easy to set up and it easy to access the money that you receive in your account from customers. However, the company has a long list of stringent rules that can see your account closed down if you violate these rules. If you plan to have a multi-tiered payment system for example for an affiliate program or if you are selling through network marketing systems, you might have to look at other payment processing options.

Google Wallet: is a Google hosted mobile application that allows users to store their credit cards and discount offers on their mobile phones and on their desktops. Both brick-and-mortar and online stores can use the Google Wallet feature to accept payments from their customers. This is an easy way for customers to carry credit cards and coupon offers and to make payments.

Amazon Payments: is an online payments solution that allows customers to buy products from your site using the information they have on their Amazon account. The platform features a code that you can easily copy and paste onto your site. It is free to set up and there are no monthly charges for merchants.

Dwolla: is a retail and peer-to-peer payment solution that enables businesses to receive payments through online transactions that do not require the use of credit cards. To incorporate this payment system into your site you will need to offer general details about your business including the tax ID number, social security number, and business location. Your account will be active once the company verifies this information.

Shopping Carts

Beside the WordPress plugins mentioned earlier in this book, some of the best shopping carts to install on your website are:

1shoppingcart: this software aggregates all the tools that you require to operate an online store. You can sell both digital and physical products, develop an email list, and follow up your leads by automatically sending them personalized emails. This shopping cart solution also allows you to integrate your site and shopping cart with social networking platforms where you can gain greater online visibility. You may also incorporate affiliate programs into your site using this tool.

E-Junkie: offers 'buy-now' tabs and shopping carts that you can easily install on your website. This shopping cart solution allows you to sell products on both your website and from other sites such as eBay, Google Merchant Centre and CraigsList, just to mention few. If you are selling downloadable products, these products are secured to ensure that they are safely delivered. If you are selling physical products, the software allows you to automatically calculate shipping costs and to manage inventory.

Magento: Magento eCommerce solutions enable merchants to process their payments and shipping modalities, to optimize their product offering at the search engines and to present site content in a way that markets the business and the products.

Product Delivery

PayPal MultiOrder Shipping is one of the most efficient methods of delivering products. The MultiOrder Shipping feature enables you to print shipping labels from your PayPal account. You may print up to 50 domestic shipping labels using this product delivery solution that uses the U. S Postal Services as the main shipping agent.

It is important that you decide from the onset whether you or the buyers will pay for shipping costs. If you choose to pay for shipping, ensure to include these costs in the products but let your customers know that you are offering free shipping. In addition, companies such as FedEx or UPS will offer you free shipping tools when you create an account with them. However, with these companies you need to guarantee that you will direct the shipping costs to customers.

Also consider **drop-shipping**. There are numerous suppliers available to assist you in sending products to customers once they buy and make payment at your site. Drop-shipping can remove the challenges of product delivery as long as you pick the right company to drop ship for you. To find suppliers I recommend checking SaleHoo, Doba, Alibaba or eSources in the UK. With drop-shipping, customers will buy products through your site and then a drop-shipping company (or a supplier) is responsible for sending the products to your customers.

Refunds

Establishing a meaningful refund policy can help build trust between you and customers. A good example is Zappos that offers a 365 days money back guarantee for its customers. You can incorporate various types of refund policies into your online business. These include:

1. An exchange-only policy allows customers to return a product if it is defective and to have it replaced by a similar or different product of the same value.

2. Store credit policies allow customers to return products and to receive credit that will enable them to purchase a different product for the credit amount.

3. Complete refunds allow customers to have a full refund of the amount they paid when they return defective products.

Mobile Site Builder

GoMobi: is a tool that allows small and medium business to create mobile websites in just a few minutes. It is important that you make your website easily accessible through mobile and smart phones, because more and more people are using these mediums to surf the net. A tool like GoMobi is compatible with most content management systems allowing your site to appear on a mobile phone just as it would on a desktop computer.

Add Interactive Features to Your Website

One way to make your site attractive and engaging for site users is to add interactive features. One effective tool to use is Wibiya that allows you to integrate your site with social networking platforms. You can also add interactive features such as forums and chat options to allow your site users to hold discussion, comment on your product offering, and to share your site with others on various social networking platforms. This tool enables your new website and online business to gain greater visibility.

Project Management

Zoho Projects: is an online project management tool that allows for easy collaboration between teams. This tool is particularly important for large businesses and those businesses that are dealing with virtual teams. The application features a Planning and Tracking feature that enables you to meet project deadlines. It also features a Bug Tracker that enables you to find bugs on your site and to fix them. Other features include a time management-tracking tool that keeps track of work in progress.

Types of Sites

1. Ecommerce

You can create your own ecommerce store using some of the tools indicated above such as Dreamweaver and WordPress among others. You may also choose to create a store with eBay or Amazon. For your site to come alive, you require a web-host to host the site. Next, find a shopping cart software that will allow you to take customer orders, compute shipping costs and sales tax and to give order notifications. Some of the best-known shopping cart softwares that you may use are WP e-Commerce, ShopperPress, 1shoppingcart, e-junkie, and magento. Next, you need an Internet merchant account to enable users to buy products using their credit cards and other payment cards. A good place to start is with PayPal that allows any of your customers to send money through an email address and for you to easily receive these online payments.

Whether you create a store on eBay, Amazon or an independent one, ensure that you identify your niche market, properly represent your brand so that customers can link your products with your brand, and pay attention to customer service, as this is what will ultimately determine if customers will refer your business to others.

2. Informational Products

The process of creating a site for informational product is similar to creating an ecommerce site. Some products that you may sell include coaching programs, how-to guides, case studies, and reviews.

Things to consider:

a. Ensure that your site has a consistent design and theme. The header, image, logo, colors and copyright should be of a similar design.

b. Create a home page that indicates the type of products that you are offering. This should be a summary that allows visitors to navigate the site for more information.

c. Remember to optimize your pages for the search engines by making use of relevant keywords for the title, meta-tag as well as content.

d. Incorporate a contact form that allows you to follow up with customers.

e. Include a refund and shipping policy that is easily accessible by all customers and site visitors.

3. Web Apps

If you are looking to build web applications for your business, you may use some of the following tools: Conduit Mobile, Google's Apps for Businesses, App Inventor, BuildApp, Shout'Em. Alternatively, you may outsource the work to a professional web app developer. Web and mobile applications optimize site user experience, thus allowing site visitors to easily find what they are looking for on your site whether they are using a desktop computer or accessing the site through their mobile phones.

4. Services

Creating a site that offers services is similar to creating other websites. However, you are not displaying products, but advertising what you can do. As such, your website content should tell customers that you have the expertise to meet their needs and that you are flexible enough to deliver personalized results. Service based businesses usually depend on local clients, thus you need to build a site that attracts these types of clients. Using features as Google Places (now Google+ Local) and Google Offers to promote your services is a good place to start in attracting local clients to your service offerings.

5. Lead Generation

Creating a lead generation website is an efficient and cost effective way of building the all important email list that will enable you to attract prospects and convert them to buying customers. To create a lead generation website, set up the basic structure of the website and then:

a. Ensure that the copy appearing on your lead page shows that you are an expert in your niche. Offer as much information about yourself, the business and the product benefits and features. Credibility will encourage site visitors to offer their information. The most successful lead generation sites are those that combine product and services information with an attractive offer for their prospects. This can be an informational product or a complimentary service.

b. Incorporate this copy into the main page of the website. Also, use tools such as FormMail or Fantastico that will automatically email you the leads from the webpages or send the leads to a database in the host server.

c. Use a list management tool such AWeber that enables you to capture site visitors' full contact details. This tool also allows you to follow up with customers and prospects through emails.

6. Membership

A membership site is a great way of monetizing your online presence and for lead and customer generation. Here are some steps to take in creating a membership site:

a. Get a membership software such as WishListMember **or** MemberWing.

b. Develop website content. Ensure that the content is compelling enough that people will want to pay for it consistently.

c. Then, find customers by creating an affiliate program. Sites such as paydotcom.com (free account) are a good place to start for creating membership sites that feature affiliate programs. For each purchase a customer will make, you are paid instantly to your PayPal account. All it will cost you is a small fee paid to paydotcom.com plus PayPal fees. For example for a $197 sales transaction, you pay in fees a total of $8. 23. With ClickBank and 2Checkout (two other affiliate platforms) you'll be paying for the same transaction $15. 78 and respectively $11. 29 fee.

d. Give free trial products that will allow people to subscribe to your site. This allows you to give free membership in the first month and then start to bill subscribed members in the subsequent months. Paydotcom.com enables you to use the trial subscription feature on your site.

e. Make the membership fee low and then generate the most income selling your own products or affiliate products.

f. Allow other people to spread the word about your site for you. Make use of platforms such as warriorforum.com where you can link up with customers, prospects and others who can put in a good word for your site.

Chapter 4
MONEY IS IN THE LIST

List building is vital for any business establishing an online presence. A list is a compilation of all your prospects' contact information. It is by developing an excellent list that you will be able to interact personally with your prospects and convert them to long term, profitable buying customers. Here are some best practices for building a lucrative list:

Avoiding Spam

Spam is essentially unsolicited messages send to a person's email inbox. Those who spam usually send these messages to a group of people appearing on a mailing list that they bought from somewhere. This method is ineffective and illegal to use in trying to build a lucrative email list.

Note that most affiliate programs will suspend your account if they realize that you are sending spam messages. To avoid being accused of spam, include an option for users to unsubscribe from your list. Include in your emails the process with which users can unsubscribe; make these instructions clear and easy to follow. Visit the Internet Society page to get familiar with spamming regulations and to avoid the common pitfalls.

Building and Using an Opt-In Form

Creating an opt-in form is an effective method of building a money-spinning email list. When site visitors subscribe through this form, it offers you ample opportunity to inform them about your product offering, any sales and discounts and hot deals that might interest them. It is also a great way of distributing an informative newsletter that will keep your audience engaged with your business.

In creating your opt-in forms, inform your site visitors what kind of information they will receive when subscribing to your newsletter. Ensure that your opt-in form makes use of visuals that will give site visitors a vivid impression of what they are signing up for.

In your free newsletter, be sure to make the content valuable and focused on meeting the needs of your target audience. For example, offer your audience tips, guides and new information that they can use to solve their problems. Remember to include a teaser statement that lures site visitors to offer their email contacts.

In creating an email list using opt-ins, make sure that you give out as much free information as you can. However, you must have your eyes on quality otherwise, site visitors will be very hesitant to offer their email information. You can offer opt-in gifts in the form of free PDF reports, ebooks or whitepapers. Alternatively depending on your message and target audience, you can create videos or webinars and offer them free of charge.

To really develop a lucrative email list, you need to put daily effort. This way you will be able to gather a decent number of quality leads, eliminating the tendency to rely on the same leads for too long.

A great tool to use in creating opt-in forms is Wufoo. You can create an opt-in form that pops up on your website-landing page and that allows customers to find out what you are offering and why they should subscribe to it. Wufoo has a free model that allows anyone free access to their tools such as form creation. Once you create the form, it is easy to import it to your website. Wufoo gives the option of embedding the form within your site or placing it as a popup window on the website.

Sales Pages

Sales pages, also known as 'squeeze pages' or 'landing pages' are webpages that capture site visitor information such as their name and email address. This page allows you to present your offer in detail and to persuade your audience to offer their information in exchange for something that your business is offering.

As you create your sales page, make an offer that your audience cannot turn down or afford to miss. Show them what the problem is from their own perspective and then tell them that it is possible to solve this problem. Start building relationship with your audience early by showing them that you understand their needs and what you can do to meet these needs. Remember to focus the sales page on the audience, their needs, and how your product will benefit them.

As you tell your audience how your product or service will solve their problems, show them the proof. Remember that for most people "seeing is believing" and they have to be convinced that you can deliver on your promise. Use solid facts and any true reviews that prove that your product works.

Elucidate your offer using a step-by-step approach that will give your audience precise information. Avoid cluttering your sales page with too much information or superfluous promises. This will jeopardize the trust between you and the audience. Instead, market your product/service but get to the point. Provide an incentive such as a free, limited trial that allows your audience to test your promise before fully buying into it. This will prove your credibility.

Make your sales page interactive by incorporating both text and video. The video will certainly make the page come alive and will create a stronger rapport between you and your audience.

Remember to optimize and test your sales page title and content for the search engines. Use the appropriate keywords in the title, within the text body and in your video presentation too. Google Website Optimizer is an effective tool to use in testing different sales pages.

Autoresponders

An autoresponder allows you to create and send customized email messages to your subscribers to make them feel unique. Some of the best autoresponder solutions are:

AWeber: this is one of the most used autoresponder tool due to its reliability. AWeber allows you to send unlimited messages to up to 500 subscribers. Although the service is costlier than other automated email solutions, it offers ease of use, flexibility and reliability. You can try it for 30 days by pay just $1 and then pay $19 a month for up to 500 subscribers.

GetResponse: this email marketing service offers user-friendly reports with graphical presentations that assist you in optimizing your email marketing campaign. It can also send out autoresponders that will follow up with your subscribers. However, the downside of GetResponse is that it cannot send automatic emails depending on the link that site visitors click on. You can try it for 30 days and then pay $15 a month for up to 1,000 subscribers.

ConstantContact: this service is ideal for businesses looking for additional features such as multilingual and custom templates, additional hosting for images and email archiving. The service also offers a tracking tool that allows you to understand what is effective and what is not. The premium cost of Constant Contact might be the only deterrent.

MailChimp: integrates humor into email marketing by linking pages to a comical YouTube video. MailChimp offers a wide variety of reports that enable you to monitor the effectiveness of your email marketing campaign. However, some subscribers might perceive the links to the humorous video as unprofessional and distracting. It is completely free if you have less than 2,000 subscribers and send less than 12,000 emails a month.

Chapter 5
CONTENT IS KING

Content marketing is one of the most important aspects of running an online business. It involves creating and publishing content that is relevant to your target audience. This content, in the form of blogs, articles, videos and audios, white papers and reports, is essential for lead generation. The type of content that you create will also make your brand more visible and display your expertise in your niche. Here is how to get started in creating resourceful content for your website.

Types of Content

Text

Undoubtedly textual content will be the most dominant on your site, thus you must make it as compelling as possible. By offering relevant content that meets the needs of your clients you will be in a position to attract a stronger site membership or followership.

In creating your content, make it interactive by addressing issues that may be pertinent to your target audience. Anticipate the various objections and questions. Tell stories that may eliminate any objections or resistance that your customers may have. The point is to ensure that you are meeting the audience needs before you can give them any sales messages. Offering compelling information is one of the best ways of building rapport with your audience.

As you create your content use persuasion techniques that will make your audience more receptive to what you have to offer them. A good place to start is by offering free informational packages such as white papers and reports, case studies or exclusive how-to guides. These informational packages will not only show your expertise, but will also create trust between you and your target audience. Only then will they be willing to part with their contact information, become frequent site visitors and eventually buying customers.

When you create reports or white papers to give out free, make them precise but resourceful. White papers or reports of about 5 to 10 pages are ideal. Visit discussion forums or use tools such as Google Trends to come up with ideas that you can create content around. Great tools to use in creating professional covers for your reports include boxshot3d.com and virtual-cover-creator. net.

Besides offering this content on your website, it is also a good idea to distribute the content on platforms such as Slideshare, Docstoc, Calameo, and Scribd. These free platforms let other people read about your ideas and expertise and then follow you back to your site.

Images

Images not only make your website more appealing, but they can also convey messages that you want to communicate to your audience. However, be sure that you obtain and use images properly to avoid copyright infringement and the legal issues that may arise.

A great way to obtain photos for your site is by using pictures that you have taken yourself. This really adds a personal touch to the images you post on your site. However, there are alternative places you can obtain suitable images to use on your site. A good place to start is Google Images where you can look through a wide range of images. However, the images that you use from Google Images are most likely copyrighted and can be used for viewing only. You might have to contact the owner of the image to use it on your own site.

Flickr is a good resource from which you may obtain images. Some images on this platform are copyrighted and cannot be used freely on other sites, while the **Creative Commons License** protects others. This License allows you to use the images that are protected but with the requirement that you attribute the pictures to the original photographer or source.

You can also use Pinterest either to share your images or to get some that you can use on your site. Pinterest is both a social networking site and a micro blogging platform that allows sites users to display images on their pin boards and share them through repining. Pinterest can also be an effective tool in attracting traffic to your website. Both tools PicSlice or vt. cr/pinterest can be used to slice, resize or crop your images before uploading them onto Pinterest.

Do not forget to use infographics. These diagrams, images and charts help you to display content in a unique and interesting manner. However, ensure that your infographics are simple and understandable to the target audience. When choosing colors for the infographics you can use tools such as Adobe's Kuler and ColorLovers.

Make use of Mind Maps to help you present content in a diagrammatic manner for your target audience to better understand content. Mind Maps softwares allows to easily create optimized diagrams and flowcharts that can help you convey your message. These softwares also allow you to customize the diagrams by choosing different colors, styles and layouts. You can also edit, add and delete the content in the MindMaps diagrams. One efficient tool that you can use to for creating mind maps is Xmind. With this tool, you can share your ideas and content on your website. You may edit your messages and diagrams, reorganize the appearance of the topics and make additions to the diagrams. You can use the same interface to look up content on Google and drag and drop images into the map.

Audio and Video

Adding audio and video to your website is a great way to make the site interactive and interesting for site visitors. It is an effective method of presenting information in a way that site users cannot easily forget.

Make use of YouTube to create and share videos about your business and product offering. YouTube videos have the potential to attract a large audience to your site. Or use Vimeo, which is another popular video hosting site that also allows people to share their videos. Create videos that are visually appealing and resourceful for your target audience.

Another tool that you can use in the creation of videos is TubeMogul that allows you to create and upload multiple videos onto your website. This tool not only saves you time but also provides you with information about the performance of the videos across the web. You may use TubeMogul to allow your videos to be uploaded automatically on the major video sharing platforms. In addition to offering resourceful information to your target audience, entertain your audience too. Distributing humorous and entertaining content is an effective way of making site visitors engaged with your site for longer.

Creating podcasts is another interesting way of presenting information. Podcasts allow your audience to connect to you (and effectively to your business) at a more personal level. You can create and post podcasts on any topic relating to your business. However, do not create podcasts that are hard selling your product and service offering. Instead, create podcasts that are resourceful and solve your audience's needs. Great tools to use are Audacity, Blubrry and iTunes.

Have a Marketing Press Kit Ready and Get Free Publicity

To boost the consumption of your site content, you need to promote the content. Press releases are an effective channel through which you can let your target audience know about your site and what it has to offer. To get started you need to prepare a marketing press kit, which is simply an information portfolio about your business. A well-prepared marketing kit allows you present your business and your brand to the media, investors as well as potential customers in a favorable light.

You may create a marketing kit on your own or hire a professional to do it for you. Either way, ensure that the kit addresses your business's mission, the product offering, any accomplishments, awards, and processes that set you apart from other businesses in your niche.

There is a cost effective way for you to gain free publicity using the HARO (Help A Reporter Out) platform. HARO allows you to answer queries in your field that reporters might be interested in. By offering comprehensive answers to these queries, you stand a chance of having your business covered and distributed across the web network.

To get started on HARO, simply sign up with your name, email address and company name. Then you will receive up to 30 leads in your inbox, three times a day. These leads are specific to your niche and it is important that you respond adequately to the queries. With your response, you may attach your full contact information or just your website link. If a reporter is impressed by the response, they may ask you for further information and an interview. Some reporters will send you a link to where your story has featured but you can use Google Alerts to find out any mentions about your business.

Store Content Safely

Dropbox: is both a file sharing and a storage platform that uses cloud technology to back up the data on your website. This tool features a public folder that allows you to easily share files and to embed them on your site. It also utilizes LAN sync, a feature that accelerates the speed with which files are synced across a local network. This makes Dropbox the ideal platform for storing data for all your computers that are locally networked.

Google Drive: is suitable for storing large PDF files and images. You may also use this tool to store project files that you want to share with site visitors. Google Drive supports

AutoCad files, Photoshop, Adobe Illustrator and other programming markup codes. It offers space of up to 10GB allowing you to upload and save videos and large files onto your website.

Transfer Files

Sending large files across one computer to another or from one online source to your website can be difficult if you do not have the right tools. If you are looking to export and import content in the form of large images, bulky reports and audio files, consider using one of the many web based file transfer services. Some are free and some will require you to pay a small monthly fee, depending on how many files you import and export and their sizes too. Some of the file transfer tools you may use are bigfatfilesender.com, YouSendIt, WeTransfer, zUpload and Mailbigfile.com.

Check for Duplicate Content

It is important that your website feature only original and unique content. It is also a good idea to deter others from copying content from your site and using it on their sites. Copyscape enables you to determine the originality of your content to avoid plagiarism. This is especially important if you buy content or if you ask someone else to create content for your site. When you sign up with Copyscape, you can get a banner to post on your site that indicates that you use Copyscape to track anyone who plagiarizes the content. Another tool that you can use for the same purpose is Tynt Publisher, which tracks how users copy and paste content from your site. It automatically includes a back link to the original source of the content when it is pasted on another site.

Keyword Density

Keyword density is something that you need to pay attention to when creating content for your site. Keyword density is the percentage of keywords that appear in an article as a ratio of the total number of words in this article. Articles with the appropriate keyword density are more likely to be optimized for the search engines. Tools such as Keyword Density Analyzer allow you to easily compute the keyword density of the content on your site.

Import Content to Your Site from RSS Feeds

RSS feeds are important sources of information that can furnish your site with a lot of relevant content. One effective tool that you can use to aggregate RSS feeds and import content to your site is Carp Evolution. This script converts RSS feeds to HTML on your site. The tool was specifically created for Internet marketers to enable them to channel information to their websites from other sources across the web. With Carp Evolution, the content that is fed to your site is updated frequently and is optimized for the major search engines.

What to Write About

To ensure that your site has fresh and relevant information, you may use web-based platforms that will give you ideas. These include ehow, yahoo answers, mahalo, answers.com, ask.com, quora.com, about.com among others. These platforms are rich with questions and trending topics that your target audience is likely to be asking. So find questions that are relevant to your niche and then answer them by writing how-to guides, short articles and even reports. You can also use platforms such as toptenz com to write product comparisons and reviews that are unique to your niche and that may interest your target audience.

Check for Trends and Hot Topics

Tweetmeme: this free tool by Twitter allows you to aggregate the popular trends on Twitter and across the entire web. You can search content by categories so that you are able to find exactly what you are looking for. This tool not only offers you the latest trends but also allows you to share these trends with your target audience and others who are following you on this platform. This serves to attract traffic back to your site, gaining more visibility for the business and the site itself.

48ers.com: this site offers a search engine platform that makes it easy for you to find mentions about any niche that might interest you. With this tool, you can find trends based on the most recent world news, where your company has been mentioned and what people are saying about it. You may also search the trending topics on the social networking sites including Facebook, Twitter, LinkedIn, Pinterest and Google+ just to mention a few. All you have to do to use this tool is to enter a subject whose content you are looking for at the search engine and then access the results.

Google Trends: this tool allows you to use multiple search terms to find relevant content and trends. You can compare large volumes of demographics, and trends across more than one region. The tool also allows you to be specific in your search so that you can search particular categories and niches that you are following.

Google Hot Trends: provides you with a list of the trending topics and searches all across the web. When you place a query on Google, you can see the top 100 trending terms and news that might interest you. You can also get access to a graph that shows the popularity of your search terms and other terms over a period. By using the most popular and relevant search terms, you will be in a position to generate content for your website based on the latest trends.

Yahoo Clues: offers in depth insights into popular trends occurring on the Yahoo platform. Using this tool can help you discover trends and to compare the information that you receive for search terms that are relevant to you. You may also use the trending terms suggested by Yahoo. In addition to news stories trending across the web, you can also see search results in the form of charts and graphs that represent certain demographic information.

Link to Similar Content

Linking your site and the content that you offer on this site with similar content is a great way to position your site as a source of information for site users. One way that you can do this is by using Outbrain, which allows you to offer recommendations that are specific to each site visitor who reads the content on your website. The tool also enables you to rate content that you recommend to your site visitors. Outbrain does not just offer suggestions based on the similarity of the content of your website to other sources.

Instead, it offers content based on how likely site visitors will stay on your site and the ones that you connect them to.

Content Curation

As you create content for your site, you will come across a lot of information. Thus, you want to use a tool that will allow you to aggregate this content in a single interface for easy access. One such tool is Evernote that allows you to keep track of the content that you collect across the web. Evernote offers you a contacts folder among other feature, that lets you tag messages with specific keywords that will assist you to remember this content later. Another content curation tool is Pinterest, that lets you collect and share all the beautiful pictures across the web.

Chapter 6
BE SOCIAL AND ENCOURAGE INTERACTION

Participating on the social web network is an effective way of publicizing your site and your business. Once you gain the visibility and the audience, it is a good idea to encourage conversations among them. Here are some strategies to use in making your site more interactive and opening it up to your audience.

Register in Listings and Directories

Web directories and listings are platforms that aggregate information about companies and their websites and make them available to potential customers. Many web users depend on web directories and listings to find what they are looking for. As such, listing your business in such platforms has the potential of gaining you visibility especially with local customers. Most of the platforms are easy, quick and free to register with yet the returns can be significant for your business. Other than exposing your business, these listings also give you the opportunity to interact and engage with potential and existing customers. In addition, backlinks from web directories have the potential of raising your ranking at the search engines.

Make your business more accessible to the local customers by registering your site with Yelp. Simply fill out the online application forms and answer the automated call that you receive. This should take you less than 10 minutes and you will have the tools necessary to engage and interact with customers. Many people in the urban centers use this listing to find businesses that meet their needs such going out for dinner, buying clothes, and finding specific services. Ensure that your profile is complete, that you respond to customers' reviews constructively, that you post regular announcements to keep your audience engaged and do not forget to embed a Yelp badge on your website. The badge will show customers that you are on Yelp and they can read reviews about your business from other customers.

Another great listing is Google Places (now Google+ Local), which is a free platform that allows you to inform your customers about your location, business hours and the types of services and products that you offer. Your target audience will be able to find you and once they do, you can interact and engage with them at a more personal level.

Yet another valuable resource is Technocrati. This is a search engine that is dedicated to helping web users find blogs. You can register your blog on Technocrati by 'Claiming Your

Blog'. This allows other people to find you and the content that you have to offer. The more people can find your blog, the better you can engage with them on your blog platform by offering content that may interest them and receiving comments and feedback from your site visitors. Remember that it is no good having a blog or site that no one visits or interacts with regularly.

Other listings and web directories that you can make use of are SuperPages, Bing Local, Yahoo Local, MerchantCircle, AngiesList, Foursquare, CitySearch, Local.com and Manta.com.

Create Social Profiles

Social media is an essential component of making your business and yourself more available to your target audience. More and more businesses are using these platforms to gain visibility and to interact with their potential and existing customers on a more personal level.

Use **Tumblr** as both a microblogging and social networking platform. It is free and easy to join and you can get started posting short blogs pictures that are related to your business and relevant to your target audience. Tumblr allows others to follow your posts and share them with others on the same platform and in other social networking places. You too can share other people's Tumblr and give them feedback.

Facebook is one of the most popular social networking platforms with over 900 million users. Facebook is a good place to get started in making professional contacts, to reach out to your target audience and to make them aware of your site and your business. As in other social networking platforms, ensure that your Facebook profile is complete and that it tells about your business. Follow up with those in your Fan Pages and do not hesitate to bring them back to your site.

Another valuable tool that you want to use is **TweetAdder**. In addition to signing up with the Twitter platform, you should consider using this tool in managing your Twitter followership and the messages that they send to you. TweetAdder can add up to 100 people into your account, allowing you to grow your following and thus remain interactive with like-minded people. The tool also enables you to send your follower automated messages but in a way that will not annoy them. This is particularly helpful as it saves you time, but allows you to stay in touch with your audience.

Other social networking platforms that you should consider engaging with are LinkedIn, Pinterest, Google+, StumbleUpon, and YouTube.

Tools such as Bit. ly, backtype, Klout enable you to track the impact that your social networking is having. By using these tools, you can track the number of clicks that your URL receives from the social networking sites where you post your links. You can also track user activity with regard to how often they click the links on your blog. This give you an idea of what draws them to your site or blog and what type of content engages the readers.

Add Social Sharing Buttons to Your Site

Adding social sharing button to your site simply makes your content sharable across the social networking sites. The more people can share your content, the greater visibility that your site and business will gain. Remember that there are millions of users on these social networking platforms and today this is how businesses are being noticed.

Most social sharing sites will provide you with a code that you can then embed on your site's HTML. This process is simple and does not require extensive HTML programming knowledge. Simply go to your site dashboard and begin to edit the HTML code from here; install the social sharing button for it to become visible on your site.

The best location to place the social sharing buttons is where they are visible and the site visitors do not need to scroll down to find the buttons. Also it is a good idea to use only those buttons that your site visitors are likely to click on. Find this out by analyzing your main source of traffic; if it comes from LinkedIn for example, then you want to include a LinkedIn share button on your site. Other essential social sharing buttons are Twitter, Facebook, Pinterest, Google+, StumbleUpon, and YouTube. To avoid cluttering your page with social media buttons consider using a service such as AddToAny or ShareThis. This will streamline the social media buttons and place them at one visible corner of your site.

Encourage Interaction through Reviews and Forums

Forums or message boards offer your site visitors a platform to interact with one another, to hold discussions and to provide opinions about various topics. By opening up your site like this, you are allowing site visitors to establish a rapport with you. This is particular important if you are looking for loyal followership for your site and subsequently your business.

A versatile tool to use in creating social networks and forums is Ning. This is a web-based service that allows you to create your own social network. This platform now has 37 million users and an upward of 1. 6 millions social networking networks. You can create a network based on different niches and the members of your social network can engage in conversations, create their own profiles, send messages and install third party application on their profiles. Use Ning to get customer feedback about your product offering, an article that you shared with them and generally, what they think of your brand. You can also use this platform to encourage those in your network to hold discussions on certain topics that may or may not relate directly to your business.

You can use several site review plug-ins but whichever you use, ensure that the output is supported by Google rich snippet program. This will allow you to submit you website for Google to review and index the site based on the reviews. Some tools and widgets to use are Zagat (for restaurant reviews), WordPress Review Site plug-in and Alexa Reviews widget.

One approach to take in creating your site is to write your own reviews. If you are selling products or services for someone else, it is a good idea to use them and then write a review for your site visitors. However, a more preferable approach is to allow user generated reviews to feature on your site. This will encourage site users to interact with you and among themselves. Hold review contests to encourage people to submit reviews to your site. Use social media platforms such as Twitter and Facebook to publicize the contest. However, make sure that you are not giving out incentives for people to write false reviews. Remember, though, that reviews can make or break your online business. You need to moderate the reviews on your site. This does not mean that you filter out criticisms or negative comments. It means that you attempt to moderate reviews that are 'spammy' or those that are simply false.

Host Webinars

Webinars are a great and interactive method of engaging your target audience. They not only educate, but they also entertain the audience. In fact, webinars can be more effective in sending out a message and interacting with customers compared to a site that features just textual content. Even as you interact with your audience, webinars can help you in your marketing campaigns albeit subtly.

Webinars have a way of engaging those who are really interested in your niche and the subject that you are presenting to them. If you are successful in engaging your audience in this way, then it is likely that you will shorten the sales cycle.

GoToWebinar: is a helpful tool that allows you to hold online webinars and to interact with your audience regardless of their location. To get started, you need to download the software from the official site, and then begin to create your webinar from there. When using this platform you will start by entering information about what the webinar is about. Then, go ahead and invite your target audience to attend the webinar; you have the option of sending them invitations through email or you can get creative by linking the invitation to the social networking sites that you participate in (Twitter, Facebook, Pinterest, Google+, etc.). GoToWebinar allows those you have invited to register to attend your webinar online. There is also a feature that enables you to remind your attendees about the webinar. You can even test your online presentation before airing it.

Google+ Hangouts and specifically **Google Hangout on Air** is also another effective tool to use in hosting live video conferencing. On this platform, you can broadcast your presentation and engage with as large an audience as you want. When the presentation comes to an end it is automatically saved into your YouTube account from where you can edit the video and then publish it and share it on YouTube. From your YouTube channel, viewers will be able to share the video across the web.

Contests, Surveys and Loyalty Programs

Contests, surveys and loyalty programs can be an effective way of encouraging online conversation and creating buzz for your business. Make use of contest to generate feedback from your customers and to improve your return on investment for your online marketing campaign. You can also expand your email list by holding these contests and surveys.

As you get started with your online contests, ensure that you set out goals concerning what you want to achieve from the contest. You should hold a contest because you want to enhance a certain metric such as improving sales, increasing your Twitter followers or Facebook fans, gaining greater visibility, just to mention a few.

Also, think carefully about your target audience and the type of contest that might really engage them. Are they tech savvy, what their age group is likely to be and what are their interests and likes. These questions will enable you to attain the contest's goals while at the same time engaging the participants. Additionally, ensure the ultimate prize is something that your target audience would anticipate to win.

Some tools to use in conducting online contests are Cubio, Strutta, BuddyMedia, and Votigo.

Consider using online surveys to engage with your customers and to show them that their feedback is important for the growth of your business. Online surveys, if well constructed, can serve as a source of detailed feedback. Keep the online surveys short to genuinely engage your target audience.

Make use of free online survey tools or commercial ones, depending on the extent of your survey. SurveyMonkey is free for up to 10 questions and 100 responses per survey. It is a good tool to use as it allows you to create surveys related to your business and target audience in just a few minutes. You can then view the results in graphical presentation, and in charts. This platform also gives you access to an audience that you can survey, according to your niche and the goals of your survey.

Lastly, online loyalty programs can be a valuable method of engaging customers in your business by rewarding them and encouraging them to become repeat customers. For you to have success in your loyalty program, you need to determine customers' value before you can engage them in the loyalty program. Nevertheless, the bottom line is that the customer value is how much profits a customer brings to your business and thus how much efforts and resources you should put in attracting them and retaining them. An excellent platform to start with your loyalty program is Punchtab.

Use SMS, Group Messaging and QR Codes

Sending out a group message is a cost effective method of communicating with your target audience. It also allows those in your group to send out messages to each other and to easily reach the wider group. This is a great way of keeping the audience engaged and up to date with relevant happenings. You can send messages as diverse as incentives you are offering in your business, a call to action or simply a reminder about an upcoming webinar.

Some great tools to use for group messaging include are groupme.com, dotgo.com, cbfsms.com and smsbug.com.

Creating and offering QR codes can also help your audience stay in touch with each other and to be connected to multimedia resources. QR codes are like the barcodes used in retail shop. You can use tools such as goQRme to create a QR code that connects users with each other and to websites, text messages and phone numbers that might be relevant to them. Users of your QR code can share content as diverse as ebooks, video and audios and links to webpages. You may use a tool such as Likify to create QR codes that connects users' mobile users to a 'like' button on your Facebook interface. This simplifies the process of linking your audience with others on Facebook. You can use QR codes at the back of business cards, marketing materials, restaurant menus and retails receipts.

Test Your Product before You Launch It

Testing your product before you launch it gives you insights into how well your target audience will receive and respond to the products. User testing tools such as Mechanical Turks allow you to spend little money to gain detailed information about your product.

Mechanical Turks (MTurks) is a tool offered by Amazon that allows businesses to conduct a semblance of surveys to determine the effectiveness of a product. By submitting tasks to a group of people (also known as Human Intelligence Task) or surveys, you will be able to receive feedback that you cannot otherwise receive from computer-generated information. In return, you pay the users a small fee for each question they answer. For you to be successful in testing your product with MTurk, it is recommended that you make your tasks or surveys precise.

Interview People in Your Industry

Video interviews are an affordable and effective means of interacting with your clients. One such tool is Skype, a communication software that allows you to communicate with others via video, regardless of the geographical location.

Another tool that you can use to hold free conferences online with clients, business investors or associates is . The tools will save you a lot of overhead costs while at the same time staying interactively engaged with your target audience.

To make the most of these communication platforms, ensure that technical aspects such as Internet connection, cameras and headphones are in place.

Provide Customer Support

ZenDesk: is a web-based customer service software that allows businesses to manage customer complaints and inquiries without the need to spend too much on customer support. The tool offers a ticket management system and a self-service platform. Upon signing up with ZenDesk, you get access to tools that enable you to support your customers and to engage them at the same time. Some of the tools that you receive include web contact forms, community platform and a repository that is knowledge-based and that can be used immediately.

ZenDesk works with your email automatically, allowing you to spend less time retrieving customer emails and more time engaging with the customer. You can make use of various forms of customer engagement. You can have private conversations that are supported by using tickets or conduct a public conversation that is accessible to the community on your ZenDesk platform.

Chapter 7
ADVERTISE YOUR PRODUCT AND SERVICE OFFERING TO YOUR TARGET AUDIENCE

After bringing your business online, you need to advertise your product and service offering to your target audience. One advantage of online advertising is that is does not have to cost you too much if you do it strategically and from a point of knowledge. You have access to numerous platforms that allow you to advertise your brand; make good use of them to improve your visibility and your return on investment

Pay Per Click Programs

Pay per click (PPC) advertising is a cost effective method of advertising your business to a wider audience. If targeted, this type of advertisement can convert prospective clients into buying ones.

AdWords: is Google's PPC advertising platform. To advertise with Google you need to simply set up an AdWords account, and select keywords that are relevant to your business. The process entails bidding for keywords and key phrases, with the highly competitive keywords and phrases costing more than the less competitive ones. Once you choose your keywords, it is time to create your compelling ad copy to tell your target audience what your business is offering. With Google, your ads will appear on the Google search networks (search pages) or on websites that are relevant to your product/service offering (content network). The advantage of PPC platforms such as AdWords is that you only pay when someone clicks on your ad and is directed to your website. For you to successfully launch your ads and for them to gain higher page rankings, the ad needs to demonstrate quality as per Google's Quality Score index.

Yahoo Advertising: is arguably the second largest platform in online advertising and search marketing with about 22% of the Internet searches share. Yahoo has introduced a new feature onto their pay per click platform, Panama. As in Google, you need to set up an account to get started with Yahoo Search Marketing. The new feature, Panama, marks a break from Yahoo's old online advertising platform. The new program offers advanced geo-targeting so that businesses can advertise to targeted markets for example U. K or Canada. Businesses can also advertise to a targeted city or its surroundings. The old system was designed to advertise brick-and-mortar businesses within a limited geographical setting. Yahoo also offers an assist and enhanced analytics feature. The enhanced analytics feature enables businesses to track the assist feature, which helps businesses to access up to 30 high converting keywords. The assist feature allows businesses to get a clearer picture of site visitor behavior and thus to invest in keywords with the highest conversion rates.

Bing: is fast becoming a formidable player in search marketing. Most small businesses looking to overcome the competition on Google use Bing.

Bing is Microsoft's search engine and to advertise on it you need to sign up for an account at the **Microsoft AdCenter**. Bing can be effective in advertising to a targeted market because the service is limited to a few countries including Singapore, U. S. , U. K. , and Canada. Unlike Google, Bing has only two language options, French and English. Although Microsoft plans to include other countries, this platform still offers an excellent opportunity to target your advertisement to audiences in these few countries. Bing allows you to increase your bid by 10% if the targeted searcher is of a certain age category and up to 20% if the targeted searchers are women.

Note: Bing and Yahoo came together in mid 2009. This means that your ads will appear on both platforms and their content network partners including Wall Street Journal, CMBC and FOX Sports, thus reaching a greater audience.

Facebook: social ads are a novel way of advertising to a large number of people all at once. This is a progressively growing social networking platform with over 400 million active users and offers a great opportunity to advertise your business. The Facebook pay per click program allows you to place small ads on the right side of users' Facebook interface. An advantage of Facebook's advertising platform is that you can choose to whom you want your ads to be visible. You can do this by choosing from various variables including age, education, relationship status, gender, geographical location, education and relevant tags and keywords.

Similar to **Google AdWords**, **Facebook** Advertising involves bidding for keywords and competing with other advertisers to have your ads featured on the Facebook platform. Facebook allows you to pay on a cost per click basis or cost per a thousand views basis. Most research indicates that cost per click offers the greatest return on investment.

Daily Offers Platforms

Daily offers can be an effective method of advertising and attracting customers to your new business. These programs enable you to offer discounted deals in return for exposure and promising customers or subscribers. Some of the most popular daily offers programs are:

Groupon: offers unique deals in that for an offer to become valid, a specific number of people must buy it first. In this way, Groupon is able to make some money and businesses have the certainty that a certain number of people will subscribe and buy the offer. When you sign up your business for Groupon's daily offers, you will not incur out of pocket expenses; you will only pay when customers buy the coupons. A strong point of Groupon is that they play a big role in advertising and promoting your business' offer. Although Groupon can be a great method of attracting new customers, it is a good idea to analyze how the move to offer daily offers using this method might affect your business' bottom line. Keep your eyes on the price point to ensure that the customers you attract will be willing to spend more on other undiscounted products.

Google Offers: is Google's daily offers program in which Google helps you create a deal and to determine the price and the methods of promoting the deal. The main features in a Google Offers advertisement include the headline, which is optimized for the search engines and to reflect what your offer is about. The ad/offer also features an image of your products and a write up that describes the product. Google will then help you to advertise this offer on their Google Offers website, email contacts and provide mobile applications to local customers who are interested in a similar product as what your business offers.

CraigsList: is a free marketing and advertising platform from which you can display your product offering to your target audience. This platform is especially helpful for Internet marketers and advertisers looking to target a wider audience on a low budget. To get started on CraigsList you need to create an account. Most advertisers do not create an account but for easy maneuvering of the platform, it is essential that you do.

CraigsList is designed for local advertising. As such, you need to limit the areas from which you are offering the product or service. Posting on more than one geographical area will get your account closed. Then, choose a category that best suits you product/service.

Avoid obvious advertising on CraigsList, as this will get your post suspended. Instead, list the products or services your business offer. Then, include some photos and prices and instruct interested prospects how they can contact you.

Chapter 8
PARTNER WITH OTHERS

Working with meaningful partners is the cornerstone of business success. As you grow your online presence, you will find that partnering with other businesses and individuals makes operating your own business much easier. With partnerships, you will learn new ways of managing a profitable business and you will be exposed to even greater opportunities. Here are some strategies to apply in finding and creating meaningful business partnerships:

Business to Business Online Partnerships

Business-to-business partnerships are collaborations between you and others in your industry or niche area. In the online world, partnerships entail the relationship between two or more webmasters who work in tandem to promote each other's business. You will enjoy mutual benefits when you can collaborate with other businesses that offer products or services that complement those that you offer.

One benefit that you will enjoy is greater visibility. By accommodating another business partner on your website, you will be surprised at how visible and accessible your website can become. When you offer complementary products and services, more customers are likely to visit your website than, if you were just selling a single product. This is especially true if as a small business, you collaborate with a more established and well-known business. Brand association with a business that is already doing well has the likelihood of boosting your own brand and subsequently, your business sales.

Moreover accommodating the products and services of another business will add more content to your website. This will make your site more informative, interactive and will enhance site visitors' experience.

Working with Affiliates

As your online business grows, consider creating an affiliate-marketing program. This approach will enable you to collaborate with professional marketers who will promote and market your product offering.

Affiliate marketing enables you to expand your brand's online presence by working with affiliates who operate niche sites that attract a specific market. Affiliation can be beneficial for both you and your affiliates.

There are literally thousands of affiliate programs (**Commission Junction**, **ShareASale**, **LinkShare**, **Affiliate Window**, **ClickBank**, **PayDotCom**, etc.) online today, thus as you create yours you need to make it unique enough to attract successful, professional affiliate marketers. Your niche market is that which you are in, so the next step is to look for websites that have site visitors who might be interested in your product offering. The offer that you provide your affiliate partners should benefit both cf you.

Create meaningful and creative promotional material that will help your affiliate partners in marketing your product/service. By making the work easier for your professional affiliate partners, you will make them more motivated to promote your offering.

Finding the Influencers

More and more businesses are seeing the importance of partnering with people such as celebrities, bloggers and journalists who have great social influence online. These influencers can have a great impact on your business when they endorse your brand or spread word of mouth information about your products.

An effective tool to use in finding influencers in your niche is **Klout**. This tool assesses a person's influence on the basis of their ability to trigger an action. Some metrics of influence that Klout uses include:

- **True reach:** this is the number of people that act on a person's content.

- **Amplification**: the frequency with which a person's content is shared. The most influential people are those whose content is commented upon and shared regularly.

- **Network**: this metric shows how well connected a person is; this is seen by how many other influencers respond to his content and share it.

Klout generates this information from other social networking sites including **Twitter, YouTube, Foursquare** and **Instagram**. It assigns a score rating the most influential people in a given niche, with 20 being the average and 100 being the highest.

WeFollow.com: This effective tool allows you to find people who create and promote meaningful content. It is also excellent in enabling you to find people who you can make aware of your tweets on Twitter. WeFollow.com allows you to follow top people on Twitter in your own niche area; you can then start to build relationships by following their tweets and encouraging them to follow yours. This tool only allows you to create three hash tags in one search for example #online marketer, #blogger, #social entrepreneur to find the influential people in these niches. This limitation minimizes spamming and cluttering of the directory.

Google+ Ripples: is a an interactive diagram that lets you see how your content is spreading and getting distributed by site users and the contacts in your social circle. You can access the Ripple diagram from the drop down menu located right of the post whose ripple effect you are monitoring. This diagram also lets you see the people who are sharing your content the most (Influencers) and the time period that the content was shared. You can use this information to make a connection with the influencers, if you have not yet done so. This data can be seen for both, your posts or the posts of those that you followed and shared them with you.

Making Use of Reward Programs

In addition to building partnerships with businesses, you can also engage your target audience, fans and existing customers. One way to do this is through a rewards or loyalty program. An excellent service to use is **FanGager**, which addresses the need for businesses to identify their greatest fans and how to engage and reward them. Today, brands such as Orange, Nokia and American Express are using FanGager.

FanGager assesses your business' social media activity and then collates the activity of your fans. Other pieces of information that this service helps you gather include your fans' interests, geographical location and demographics. This information allows you to create games, contests, online credits and prizes to be won by the most positively active fan on these social media platforms. Fan activity is most based on how often they interact with your brand's pages on platforms such as Twitter and Facebook.

Exchanging Opinions and Expertise

As a sprouting small online business, it is important that you engage with other entrepreneurs to find solutions to problems and available opportunities. A platform such as **Sprouter**.com allows you to easily network and communicate with other online entrepreneurs about all aspects of business. Sprouter.com is a social media platform that works on a similar concept as Twitter. This tool offers you instant access to your pages and profile and notifies you of messages you receive from other users. If you are looking to spread the word about any aspect of your business to fellow webmaster, then tools such as Sprouter.com can prove to be effective.

An important aspect of partnership is strategic link sharing and exchanging. Sprouter.com allows you to showcase your expertise through content sharing. This will position you as the go-to person in your niche and other influential online entrepreneurs will be eager to follow you. When these influential online entrepreneurs tell others about your content, your site will attract a lot of backlinks and traffic, which is every online marketer's aspiration.

Chapter 9
MONITOR AND TRACK GROWTH

Plenty of changes will take place in your online business on a daily basis. New people may visit your site, your social activity will vary from time to time, and different people will click through your ads. To keep track of how well you are doing and how effective your online activities are, you need to monitor and track growth. Depending on the metrics that you are looking to measure, various tools are available to you. Here are some to get you started:

Google Alerts: is a free tool that allows you track what is happening across the web based on a keyword of your choice. You can also use this tool to monitor where you or your brand are being mentioned across the web. Getting started on Google Alerts is simple. Head over to the main page at **http://www. google**.com/**alerts** and then fill out the short form that allows you to create alerts according to your preferences. Add your company name and email, and then select the 'Comprehensive' and 'as-it-happens' options. After this initial set up simply use the platform by inserting a keyword that will generate the specific information you are looking to monitor. For optimal results, consider using phrases. This is especially applicable if you offer more than one product/service. Simply insert quotes around the phrases and you will receive alerts on exact matches.

Using negative keyword will enable you to narrow down your search and thus generate results that are more specific. This works by placing the (-) symbol next to a search word so that results that are not directly related to that keyword will not appear in your searches. This is especially helpful for example, if some of your products have a similar name to another object or person.

Google Analytics: allows you to track a wide range of data about you website, enabling you to make the changes that are required to optimize your site. Start by setting your Analytics account at the main page. You will receive a code to apply on your website HTML and then create a profile for your business site(s). Follow the systematic process that is availed to you; this will help you create a script to embed on your site. Some of the metrics that you can track and measure are:

- **Visitors**: you can track the number of people visiting your site, their geographical location, their language, the browsers they use to reach your site and the number of times these visitors access you website.

- **Sources of traffic**: you can determine how people find your site and track the keywords and links that bring people to your webpages.

- **Content information**: you can measure how well your content is optimized for the search engines. You can also determine the most popular pages, how people reach these pages and how they exit.

- **Goals**: this feature allows you to see user behavior and if it meets the objectives, you had set. Some trends that you can track include subscription rates, purchases and downloads.

- **Online commerce:** you will be able to monitor trends such as the sale of your merchandise, revenue and other financial transactions.

Klout: is a tool that measures your influence on various social networking sites including **Twitter**, **Facebook**, **YouTube**, **Instagram** and others. Klout has several features such as **Klout Score** that can help you measure the effectiveness of your social media campaign. High scores of 30 and above indicate that your campaign is effective, while a lower score below 30 means that you need to improve your social marketing strategy. If you hire a social marketing company, you can measure how well they are performing with regard to your social media campaign. This can help you determine whether it is still worthwhile to keep investing in this company.

If you are looking to enhance your Klout Score it advisable that you create compelling posts. People are more eager to share creative and interesting posts and the more they do, the high your Klout Score becomes.

Tweet. Grader.com: your **Tweet. Grader** allows you to measure how well you are using the Twitter platform for marketing. A Tweet Grade is a percentage score determined by how effectively you implement Twitter best practices for business compared to other graded Twitter users. Some factors that affect your Tweet Grade include the number of followers you have, the influence of the people who are following you, the number of people that you are following, how well you update your network and how often your network shares your tweets.

Zoomsphere.com: is yet another tool that enables you to track the impact you are having with your social marketing campaigns. This tool display data in graphs and charts representing trends in major social networks including **Facebook**, **Twitter**, **LinkedIn**, **Google+** and **YouTube,**

and allows you to see the mentions that you are receiving across social networks. Signing up for an account is free. Then, add your profile and a link to your site or other social networking platforms and then measure the impact that you are having on these networks.

PinReach.com: is an analytic tool that allows you to measure your business' influence on Pinterest. PinReach offers insights on various statistics about your account including the number of pins and repins, how many people liked your pins and the number of followers you have. Other metrics that you can access pertain to the comments and community boards. You can set up your PinReach account through your Twitter or Facebook accounts or with your email address. Then, integrate this tool with your Pinterest account to allow PinReach to automatically aggregate data from your Pinterest board.

Throughout this book I have shown you that not all online business tools need to cost the earth. I have also shown that some of the best tools and resources out there are actually free. Taking the first steps towards setting up and launching your online business can be a daunting task. Not only can the world of online marketing be scary and confusing, it can also be extremely costly with little return on investment when done ineffectively.

The tools, links, resources and tips that I've covered off in this book should really help you on your journey to success. Not everything in the world of online marketing needs to cost money. It is also possible to implement a successful strategy with some dedication, hard work and an understanding of the right tools to use and the costly ones to avoid.

I wish you every success in your venture and believe that this book will help you on your journey. What I would also add at this stage is that you shouldn't always limit yourself to everything you read in books and on forums. There are literally thousands of tools out there and many more different ways of implementing an online strategy. Take advice from professionals like myself but don't stick rigidly to what people tell you. Find what works well for you and disregard what doesn't.

Thank you for reading my book. I hope you enjoyed it and found it extremely useful, whether as a consumer, a small business owner or as an online marketing professional. I write my books with a lot of dedication and from the heart. I have a passion for online marketing and for supporting and encouraging others to make the changes that can grow their online business. Online marketing is an ever-evolving industry and, as such, keeping up with the latest trends can be challenging. My books are written in a way that will help all businesses improve their online presence and effectiveness but my specific aim is to help small businesses, startups and those who are looking to take their business online for the first time. I have a lot of experience in the industry and I want to share my knowledge and insights with others who are looking to maximize their online potential. As well as writing books I also run my own publishing company that supports and encourages independent authors and small business owners to take their work and themselves to the world. I get most fulfillment from my work when I'm passing on tips, advice and my experience of publishing and digital marketing to authors and businesses that are just starting out on their journey.

Once again, I hope you enjoy my books and I'd appreciate any feedback. I'm always looking to challenge myself and improve the way that I work and openly encourage my readers and clients to let me know what I can do differently in the future.

If you would like to write a review, please follow one of THE LINKS below to publish your review on Amazon.

US: amazon.com/dp/B0089YNNY4
UK: amazon.co.uk/dp/B0089YNNY4
IT: amazon.it/dp/B0089YNNY4
ES: amazon.es/dp/B0089YNNY4
FR: amazon.fr/dp/B0089YNNY4

Author:

Website – www.gabriela-aylor.com

Twitter – www.twitter.com/globalndigital

Pinterest – www.pinterest.com/taylorgabriela

Linkedin – www.linkedin.com/in/gabrielataylor

Facebook – www.facebook.com/globalndigital

Gender is not primarily based on the sex of an individual. It is more of a social construction and it varies according to the different cultures. It is imperative that customers know that gender based designing and marketing has little to do with physiology and more to do with neurology. Neurology affects how individuals think, how they make decisions and how they perceive their environment.

Some men choose clothes and other items using the 'feminine' part of their brain. The same also occurs to many women and it affects how they dress and even the cars they buy. Culture also plays an important role in gender expressions. For instance, businessmen in China carry leather purses as a symbol of social status and wealth.

The neurology of a customer will definitely have a huge impact on the design process as well as the marketing procedure. The job of the marketer is to design information in such a manner that it appeals to all clients despite their different neurology. This is a tough task but it can be achieved efficiently if research is well carried out and the product is something that appeals to the clients.

The information you present to a consumer needs to illicit the desired emotion, reaction or action. You need to ensure that the client has received the information and interpreted it the way you want him or her to do so. In this respect, the clients will be in a position to take the action you want them to take.

Many customers are not really getting what they want because of the various gender stereotypes in the market today. Many marketers will market their product using these gender stereotypes, as this is the norm today. Females have to wear pink while blue is forced down the throat of men.

However, some individuals do not fall in their right category. For instance, there are boys who like to wear pink clothes. The same thing happens with many girls that like blue clothes. Clever marketers can use this to their advantage in order to increase their customer base hence more profits. Take for example women who want to own high performance sports cars. This is not normal according to what society expects women to drive. Addressing the needs of such women and many others will open a bigger market for you and your company.

Getting Customers to Buy from You

There are certain individuals who seem to be almost incapable of changing their minds. These individuals are described as being hard headed and are a nightmare for most marketers. However, this is not the case. Such individuals are constantly changing their minds and that is why they are so adamant to stick to their earlier decisions. Their minds are constantly having a second thought and then going back to the first.

Other people never seem to be able to make up their minds. It is as if they are physically incapable of making a decision and sticking to it. However, the situation is not what it seems. Such people are actually making decisions and sticking to them. They are blessed with the gift of quickly choosing the best scenario and sticking to it.

As a marketer designing a marketing plan, you should be able to identify the kind of clients you are targeting. Are your potential customers the 'Towards' kind of people or are they the 'Away From' kind of people?

The Towards category of customers are those who seem to lack the ability to make choices. These kinds of people are the easiest to work with under normal circumstances because they can simply be directed towards what they like and the job is done. However, this does not happen in this case as influencing how a Towards client thinks is a daunting task for many marketers. You have to constantly point them towards the direction you want them to take. Their minds are constantly trying to compare different scenarios and see which one suit them best. This means that you have to be there every step of the way trying to convince them that the direction they are taking is the best. Otherwise, you might end up losing very important clients.

People with the **Away From** mannerisms are the easiest to handle in this case. Dealing with them is significantly more profitable than dealing with individuals with the Towards behavior. They will come to your office or website and act as if they really do not care about the product.

A good marketer will begin to influence how such a person thinks by simply prompting the client to identify what he wishes to change. This works exceptionally well in websites where you give the client different options. These options include Color, Size, Style and many others. The client will seem to be making his own decision and sticking to it but it is really you who is guiding him or her.

These tips will help you in designing effective strategies to handle these two different types of people.

Provide the user with options from the start. This is will enhance your business performance, as most of the visitors to your website will be people with Away From behaviors. Giving these people options enables them to explore while creating a façade that they have not yet made up their minds.

Ensure that each page of the website has only one option. This keeps the clients focused and too many options do not distract them. They might end up playing with the options without actually making any final decisions.

MARKETING TO MEN

Men Show a 'Towards' Characteristic while Women Have an 'Away From' Characteristic

This generalization cannot be applied to all aspects of life as it would not hold true. However, this generalization is a fact when it comes to the designing of sites and marketing material that will catch the attention of both sexes.

In summary, it can be said that gender sensitive marketing can only be gender specific in certain circumstances.

Conclusive research carried out on different sites has come up with some interesting findings. On most sites women have a higher probability of thinking like men than the chances of men thinking like a woman.

This could be very beneficial to marketers if they take advantage of the situation at hand. This is also the reason why many sites are male gender biased. In more general terms, get to know your target audience and potential clients before actually designing for them.

It is also common knowledge that the women have a strong influence on the buying habits in many countries. For instance, in America the women control about 85% of the purchasing that goes on there. Smart marketing companies use this aspect in order to promote their products and increase their profits. They do this by designing marketing strategies that tactically target the female audience.

Businesses using social media as a tool to gain a bigger portion of the market benefit a lot. They target women who seem to have a lot of influence on what others are purchasing. Such women include mom bloggers who usually have a lot of influence as well as followers on the social media sites.

MARKETING TO WOMEN

Women are probably going to purchase goods from brands they engage with over the social media sites. Many businesses are targeting these women because of various reasons. The underlying fact remains that there are more women on the social media sites as compared to men. According to statistics carried out on Facebook, the women participate more than the men do by about 55%. This is not surprising but it is a major strong point that many businesses need to exploit.

In order for companies to reap the most out of targeting women with their marketing strategies, a few things should be noted. Men and women are very different not just in the physical sense but also in their thinking patterns. Marketers should consider these differences, as they will assist in shaping the most effective marketing strategy. We have already identified that women are more engaged on social media sites than men are. This therefore means they have the biggest effect in the market.

One thing you probably know already is the fact that women are strategic purchasers while men are immediate buyers. Men see something they like online and their first instinct is to buy the item. Many of them do not consider its usefulness after sometime among other considerations. They get an impulse to buy and they just click buy.

Women on the other hand have many questions running through their minds before making an actual purchase. The answers to these questions are the main determinants of whether the woman will purchase the item or not. If you think strategically, you will be able to provide the answers these women want in order to convince them to buy the item. Remember many women have the Away From mentality while the men have a Towards attitude.

Women want to know that if they purchase an item online it will be able to meet their current needs as well as their long-term needs. Research also indicates that women are more concerned about future usefulness as opposed to the current usability. In addition to this, women are prone to remain loyal to a particular brand even long after the initial purchase. They are even more likely to spread the word about how good the brand is to others through the social media sites. This could have a huge impact on the number of customers your company has as well as your revenue base. It is essential that you and your company strive to get these recommendations.

Research shows that about 37% of women are on social media sites in order to gain information about a particular brand or product. They are constantly scheming through product reviews to analyze whether the product is as good as the marketers say it is. They also follow these brands in order to receive first hand information on coupons, promotions and special offers being offered by the company.

To fully exploit the social media experience, try to humanize the website as much as possible. This is so that you can achieve having as many women followers as possible. In reference to this, it is good to know that all women need a personal touch to their online experience. If you are able to add this to your strategy, it will surely give out good results.

Use Different Approaches for Different Women

When designing a marketing strategy it is vital that you recognize that not all women are the same. Different women have different tastes, preferences and interpret information differently. Not forgetting that the women have different ages as well as backgrounds. It is wrong to assume that if you design just a general strategy targeting all women in general it will work. This is only a recipe for disaster for you and your business.

The approach you use should be able to encompass all the different women there are who might be interested in your product. Make them interested and ensure that they stay that way. Strive to make your product as well as your site a daily part of their lives.

It is estimated that nearly 46% of all women check their smartphones every morning when they wake up. 31% of women check their computers for new information or trending topics on social media sites such as Twitter. This clearly indicates that if you want to gain a huge following you need to have a strong and effective mobile marketing campaign.

Other important determinants of how well your strategy will be accepted include age and demography of the women you are targeting. A woman's age will influence how she should be approached in terms of the marketing strategies to be applied.

This clearly influences the approach you as the marketer are likely to use in order to get access to your desired age group. This means that you need to know exactly the age group you are targeting. In addition to this, it is reported that many working ladies are the ones who look for information from their smartphones. On the other hand, stay at home mums or wives are most likely to use their computers for the same purpose.

There are various channels you can use in order to access your target audience. All channels seem to intertwine. This should prompt you to use all channels to spread your message. If a woman sees your message or brand repeatedly in the various channels she uses, she is more likely to remember the product and the brand.

There is a lot of information that marketers need to have at their fingertips in order to effectively infiltrate the women market. Amazingly, this market is worth over $7 trillion in America. The situation replicates itself in many countries in the world.

Many big companies have used these tips successfully. One tip that businesses should utilize is being able to identify exactly the type of women who are likely to buy the product they are selling. Many companies often overlook this fact despite it being key to the success of any marketing campaign.

Women need to feel that their own individual needs will be met when they purchase an item. They are more likely to feel this if the marketing strategy adopted reaches out to them on a personal level. One company that has taken time to research about the type of women it is targeting is the Salomon Ski company. The company is now boasting of the higher annual sales mainly due to the increase in clients many of whom are women.

Another common mistake made by many start up or small businesses is creating a different brand for the women customers. This works only in a few circumstances and the women at times feel left out of the experience all together. The companies are doing this in a bid to focus more of their energies on the boy brands. These companies do not realize that this is a waste of money. Just make a product that can be used by both sexes without any discrimination.

One company that has managed to do this with relative ease is Apple. More and more women are purchasing iPods throughout the world. This is because the device is not biased according to sex.

As we have seen previously in this book, it is absolutely vital to understand the audience and demographics that you are targeting whilst also being as inclusive as possible to maximize your potential customer base. Not only should age and generation be considered, but it is key that you also look at the significant purchasing differences between gender. By understanding these differences you can again ensure that you are making the most of your marketing efforts.

If you enjoyed this section of "Targeting Your Market", you can grab your copy here:

US: amazon.com/dp/B009P2HSZ4

UK: amazon.co.uk/dp/B009P2HSZ4

IT: amazon.it/dp/B009P2HSZ4

ES: amazon.es/dp/B009P2HSZ4

FR: amazon.fr/dp/B009P2HSZ4

CA: amazon.ca/dp/B009P2HSZ4

BR: amazon.com.br/dp/B009P2HSZ4

If you liked this book you may also be interested in purchasing my "Give Your Marketing a Digital Edge" series

GIVE YOUR MARKETING A DIGITAL EDGE - VOL. 1 (6-Book Bundle) – <u>www.amzn.to/10XUmzX</u>

Budget Marketing: How to Start & Market an Online Business with Little or Zero Marketing Budget: why pay for online tools when there are fantastic free ones available that will help your business for absolutely nothing?

Plan, Create, Optimize, Distribute: Your Strategic Roadmap to Content Marketing Success: by mastering content marketing, you can connect with customers on a personal level, build a relationship, call your audience to action, and provide a platform for customer feedback.

Targeting Your Market: Marketing Across Generations, Cultures & Gender: marketing by demographics can be as simple as not advertising baby diapers on a site aimed at Baby Boomers.

But the truth is there's a lot more to know if you want to maximize business success and avoid blunders.

Mobilize to Monetize: The Fast Track to Effective Mobile Marketing: when you use mobile technology to promote a brand and its products and services anytime, from anywhere, you can target your messages based on information you already have and engage your customers directly.

Advertising in a Digital Age: Best Practices for AdWords and Social Media Advertising: learn how to use online advertising to reach more people, interact with your community, collect feedback and monitor results in real-time, adjust your advertising quickly, and target and retarget your messages for relevancy all on a tiny budget.

Globalize to Monetize: Taking Your Online Business to New Markets: marketing globally requires cultural understanding and overcoming barriers of language and culture are crucial to successfully market globally.

GIVE YOUR MARKETING A DIGITAL EDGE - VOL. 2 (4-Book Bundle) – www.amzn.to/10XUmzX

Google Best Practices: How to Build and Market Your Business with Google: YouTube, Google+, Google+ Local, Google News, Google SEO, AdWords, AdSense, etc.: this book tells you how you can make money using everything Google has to offer.

Socialize to Monetize: How To Run Effective Social Media Campaigns across the Top 25 Social Networking Sites: by mastering content marketing, you can connect with customers on a personal level, build a relationship, call your audience to action, and provide a platform for customer feedback.

Pinterest Marketing - The Ultimate Guide: if your customers are on Pinterest, you need to be there too! Leverage the power of visual marketing with one of the best tools ever invented to increase sales for your business.

Tumblr for Business - The Ultimate Guide: learn how to use Tumblr to showcase your brand to a worldwide audience, create social buzz, and take your business to the next level.

WANT TO GET PUBLISHED?

It is often said that everyone has at least one book in them in their lifetime. Ever wanted to write and publish a digital or paper book but don't know where to start?

That's where Global & Digital (www.globalndigital.com) come in. We publish both fiction and non-fiction and we will edit and format your manuscript, design your cover, convert for publishing and distribute your book for you and also run your promotional campaigns. We can even arrange for an audio book recording or translate your book and cover into a number of different languages. We provide assisted self-publishing services for independent authors allowing you to take your book and get it published easily and affordably in a wide range of different formats. We are not a traditional publishing house, but instead provide authors with support and expertise. As such, all the profits you make from future sales of your books will be yours.

We have many years of experience in Digital Marketing, Writing and Publishing allowing us to offer our unique range of professional services. **Check all our services at www.globalndigital.com and let us take your work to market!**